AUDIBLES

AUDIBLES
MY LIFE IN FOOTBALL

JOE MONTANA
AND BOB RAISSMAN

WILLIAM MORROW AND COMPANY, INC.
NEW YORK

B
Montana

Library of Congress Cataloging-in-Publication Data

Montana, Joe, 1956–
    Audibles : my life in football.

    1. Montana, Joe, 1956–   . 2. Football players—
United States—Biography. 3. San Francisco 49ers
(Football club) I. Raissman, Bob. II. Title.
GV939.M59A3   1986   796.332′092′4 [B]   86-12591
ISBN 0-688-06298-9

Printed in the United States of America

First Edition

1 2 3 4 5 6 7 8 9 10

BOOK DESIGN BY PATRICE FODERO

For Jennifer, Alexandra, Joe Senior, and Theresa. All my love and appreciation.

—J.M.

For Monroe, Doris, and Laurel. Thanks for being there.

—B.R.

Acknowledgments

Every quarterback needs a good team supporting him. I was fortunate to have a good one alongside me during this project.

I'd like to give my sincere thanks to Bob Raissman for sticking to this project since January 1985. I would also like to thank Larry Muno for bringing the authors together.

My deepest thanks to Lisa Drew for her guidance and patience with us.

I would also like to thank the following people who helped along the way: Jerry Walker, Michael Zagaris, Deborah Baker, Larry Moulter, and Pat Sloan Hunt.

Joe Montana

Contents

Introduction

This is an unusual day at our training camp in Rocklin, California. We're between practices and my two biggest fans are with me. My wife, Jennifer—or as the newspapers call her, "the beautiful Wilhelmina model Jennifer Wallace"—and my mom, Theresa, are both here. If I was a rookie, I would be taking some shit from the guys about having my mom at training camp.

The heat is pretty bad here at Sierra Community College, and it's lulled the three of us into a light sleep on the lawn near the players' dorm. We're all relaxed, enjoying this noontime siesta. I'm more than relaxed. Mom and Jen may be sleeping lightly but I'm passed out, dead asleep.

"Joe, Joe," Jennifer says, "Wake up! Joe there's a snake coming at us." I jump up and so does Mom. A boa constrictor someone let out of the science building is wriggling our way. What's happening now? Can it be raining? What's going on? The automatic sprinklers are soaking us. Welcome to training camp, San Francisco 49er style.

Rocklin is one of the hottest places on the face of the earth. Rain is such a welcome relief here that seeing a dark cloud gives me a big lift. Rocklin's a little town, a short drive from Sacramento and two hours from San Francisco. It's a long way from my home in Palos Verdes Estates, where I can look out my window and see the Pacific Ocean.

Rain is a precious commodity in Rocklin because it breaks the heat of training camp. Rain in Rocklin is as rare as snow in Miami. The beginning of a football season means heat. It also means spaghetti Americana in the cafeteria, and—of course—those lovely dorms. When I plop down in the dank, dark dorm—where a lexicographer no doubt created the word *mildew*—I sometimes think that either our coach, Bill Walsh, or our owner, Edward J. DeBartolo, Jr., took great pains to find this place.

The mythical advertisement they placed in a newspaper might have sounded something like this: MAN WANTED TO FIND HELL—AS IN HOT—ON EARTH. PLEASE SEND FINDINGS ASAP TO EDWARD J. DEBARTOLO, JR., CHAIRMAN, SAN FRANCISCO 49ERS FOOTBALL CLUB, YOUNGSTOWN, OHIO.

Mr. DeBartolo and Bill succeeded. The purpose of their mission became clearer when I stepped out of the locker room fully dressed—shoulder pads, pants, helmet, the works—at 7:45 in the morning. I walked along a concrete driveway and out onto the practice field, where the San Francisco 49ers began preparing for another NFL season. It was early in the day but the temperature was closing in on 95 degrees. Whoever found this spot found a place where the only thing a football player can do is practice, recuperate, and study the system.

While the guy was at it he also found a location where most of the food is fast—burgers and prefabricated pizza—the women are all sixteen, and the fans are so unbelievably enthusiastic that sometimes they'll fill bleachers so far from the practice field that binoculars are a necessity to see anything. For me, well, when I walk around camp I can also feel something else. I can feel, touch, and see the enthusiasm of the fans, the 49er faithful.

It starts slowly. I leave the dorm and I hear a whisper.

"Montana."

The whispers multiply.

"Montana, Montana, Montana."

The next thing I see is a swarm of kids, between the ages of four and fourteen, running as fast as they can toward me. All they want is an autograph. They're great. I love it. But when I'm through signing I can't wait to get to the old fishing hole, the swimming pool. Put on the shades, grease up, and relax. It's the only place at training camp where the guys can really loosen up.

The swimming pool is our oasis in Rocklin, the only place with any redeeming social value. Here we can get away from coaches, reporters, and sometimes even the fans. We can relax and shoot the breeze for maybe an hour a day. Believe me, it's extremely important.

Here, walk through this maze of fences, and I'll give you an inside look at life around the pool.

There's my friend Chuck Fitzpatrick, the gentleman who runs the pool at Sierra Community College. Chuck has taught me how important it is to relax during training camp. The guy lying on the raft that's big as a queen-size bed is "D.C.," Dwight Clark. You know him—he made that routine catch against Dallas in the NFC Championship game in 1982. The fellow with the shades, lying in the inner tube, is Matt Cavanaugh. He plays behind me but a lot of teams would be starting him.

Look out, I don't think you want to get splashed. That large guy on the high diving board is Russell Francis, our tight end, the man somebody once called "All World." The gent looking at him from across the pool is his dad. Sometimes I wish my dad, Joe Montana, Sr., were here, he means so much to me. Anyway, these are just a few of the guys—the rest will be down later.

Sometimes I'll just get into the pool and drift. Not just my body but my mind. It's been a very long and sometimes strange trip for me, that trip from Monongahela to the San Francisco Bay. Things haven't always been easy. Joe Montana has spent a lot of his career in a place called no-man's-land. I don't know how others refer to this situation but that's what I call it. It's a state of limbo. Not knowing whether you're coming or going. Not knowing where you stand on the team and sometimes wondering if you're handling life OK. It happened in high school, at Notre Dame, and in San Francisco until I unlocked the door in '82 when we walked out of the Silverdome as world champions. One thing I've learned about myself, as Flip Wilson once said, "What you see is what you get." I'm taking one day at a time. Sometimes I'm winning and sometimes I'm losing but nothing is premeditated.

I've done things on my own when I shouldn't have but that's the way I chose to go. I've always felt that if you believe in something you just have to go for it. Some people don't understand that. It seems that they think because I've won one national championship and two Super Bowl MVPs I hold the keys to what it takes to succeed at life. Well, maybe people have a preconceived notion of what a winner should be like. I'm just glad I don't fit that mold. I'm not the laid-back guy people say I am. I've put in a lot of time to get where I am. That time has been accompanied by a great deal of luck. It's also been helped along by many good people around me. When you get right down to it, I'm probably not a whole lot different from you, but, fortunately, your life isn't played out on a stage. When you take your wife or girlfriend out for dinner, Herb Caen, who writes a gossip column in the *San Francisco Chronicle*, isn't going to want to find out if you put French or Italian dressing on your salad. Nobody is going to take the trouble to concoct weird stories or rumors that hurt you, your friends, and your family. Sometimes I wish that Jen and I could just be left alone.

I have this fantasy about privacy. I think of a man named Christopher Cross. Remember him? He was a singer, a heavyset guy with a high voice, who won a bunch of Grammy awards a few years back. I hear he's driving race cars now. Well, Chris didn't tour. He went in the studio and recorded his hits; his picture didn't even appear on his albums. Chris just did his job and that was it. So why not football without fanfare? Now that would be the way to go. No interviews, no people to meet, nobody trying to pick my brain. But when we won that Super Bowl in 1982 my life changed forever.

I'm getting used to it all now, but down here at the pool is a place to escape, one of the few times during a season when I can relax. Let's take a dip, because you and I have a lot of ground to cover. Now, everybody in the pool.

—JOE MONTANA,
Rocklin, California,
August 1985

Beginnings

During my junior year at Ringgold High School, I received recruiting letters from almost every major college in the country, including Notre Dame, where, in the back of my mind, I knew I was going to go. My father wanted me to go there and he had done so much for me throughout my early career that I didn't want to disappoint him.

But it was more than that. I wasn't a fool. I knew if I could do well at Notre Dame I could fulfill a lifelong dream, the dream of playing professional football. Also, because Notre Dame stressed academics, I would graduate with a significant degree. Prior to making these recruiting trips to different universities, I believed I was a pretty good football player. Once I took a look at some of the different campuses, I realized that although I had confidence in my ability, it was not going to be easy becoming a starting quarterback at a major university.

I didn't see much of the Notre Dame campus when I went to visit South Bend during a winter weekend my senior year. It was raining, and looking back, a couple of things stick out in my mind. First, I was just one of a number of good athletes the school wanted. After all, they seemed to have their pick of the lot. The Notre Dame player who was supposed to take me around to show me the sights at Notre Dame was Frank Allocco, another man who wanted to be a quarterback. Although I didn't spend much time with him, he clued me in fast.

• "Look, if you're coming here to just play football and get an easy diploma, forget it," Frank said. "If you want to do that there are plenty of other places to go. There are also places where you don't have to go to class and they'll pay you." I had never thought about that before—getting paid to play college football. Two years later I might have thought about it. But I had heard about all that fighting Irish tradition. "Another thing," he said. "There might be a few professors who'll help you here, you know, let you slide. Most of them won't. There are a lot of easier places for you to go." After that shot of reality Frank pointed me in the direction of the Morris Inn, the place where all the recruits stay. The rain continued to come down the rest of the weekend. I didn't leave the hotel.

When I entered Notre Dame the next fall, things were pretty tough. Forget about football for a moment. The course load was extremely difficult. This wasn't a school where they offered Skin Diving 1110. Everyone in the freshman class had to take required courses, no exceptions, no excuses. Now let's move to the football field. In my mind I was Joe Montana, the guy who was somehow going to impress everyone enough to get a starting role on the freshman team; I even thought I was good enough to kick some butt on the varsity. Wrong. First of all, Coach Ara Parseghian was interested in a couple of upperclassman quarterbacks: Tom Clements and Rick Slager.

Oh, I forgot to mention the fact that Ara didn't take any chances when he was betting on the Irish's future. He signed seven quarterbacks my freshman year.

Joe Montana, Jr.'s role, in the eyes of the Notre Dame coaching staff, was to come out in practice and play the role of the opposing team's quarterback. I was an actor. Maybe that's where I got my initial training for television commercials.

You want to know what plays the Fighting Irish ran that year? Don't ask me. I never had a chance to run the offense or learn the plays. Call me Practice Dummy Montana.

Needless to say, the best time I had was at practice. You take a person whose main reason for playing football is that his competitive glands are set in overdrive and reduce him to a scrub and of course he's going to love practice. It was the only chance I had to do anything. This was really paying dues. I and the others who never played knew that we were the scum of the team. If we knew it, so did the starters, and they weren't satisfied that we were scum, they were going to make sure we were scrambled scum.

If you ever wondered why I'm able to get up after Singletary or McMichael or Gastineau pounds the crap out of me, I've got the Welcome Wagon boys from my freshman year at Notre Dame to thank for that. They didn't just get off by punishing you, they loved to knock you on your butt and laugh in your face. One who was a destroyer was Mike Fanning. He never said two words on or off the field, but he hit as hard as anyone I played against. The man was scary. Another was linebacker Greg Collins. He was the ultimate. During one practice I was having some good luck. If I couldn't play in the games, I was going to try to make these guys look bad in practice.

Well, I dropped back to pass, looked to my left, and turned to throw to my right. Collins was on me. At that moment, I knew what it must be like to cross a railroad track and not see the train coming. My body felt like liquid mercury, every bone felt like a piece of jelly. I looked up, and Collins looked like that comic book character Stumbo the Giant.

"Hey, Joey, how ya feel, pal?" he said, laughing. "What's a matter kid, did I hurt you?"

I couldn't even get mad at him. He taught me a lesson. Don't ever get smug in this game. Someone is always waiting around the corner to kick your Italian butt.

2

Friends

Thank goodness for the DeCicco family.

Before I went to Notre Dame I hadn't been away from home at all. When any trips were taken it was with my mom or dad, or both. So when I arrived at Notre Dame I was really homesick and looking for friends. Nick DeCicco was my roommate and his father, Mike, was the fencing coach and the academic adviser to all the athletes at Notre Dame. Having Nick for a roommate was really important to me. Nick and I had a similar sense of humor, and we had football in common. Because of his father, he knew about Notre Dame. This gave me a sense of security.

Not playing was frustrating. I called home a lot and my father would tell me to hang in, but that was easier said than done. Although I didn't know it at the time, I was being put to the test. As my career progressed, I found out that inside any organization people are reluctant to pat you on the back. If you're not prepared to be ripped from all sides you're in big trouble.

Football was my number-one priority, but as long as I wasn't getting any game time I decided that I would try to find out what college life was all about. I tried to have as much fun as I could.

Notre Dame is different from a lot of big universities; it doesn't segregate its athletes in a jock dorm. Instead, you are thrown in with the rest of the students. But I knew the football players were different. The other students knew and I knew the football players were different. This feeling manifested itself in a few ways. The one that sticks in my mind was the fuss over our eating habits. We all ate in the same cafeteria but a lot of students thought we were getting better food than they were. Actually, the food was the same but the rules were different.

Every student could eat as much food as he or she wanted. But the nonplaying students could only get one portion at a time. The athletes could pile up on the first trip. All the students had to dish their salads from a big bowl into a little one; the athletes had theirs premade. This system made good sense. Can you imagine a guy like Willie Fry, a big defensive end for us during my years at Notre Dame, being forced to run back and forth to fill his plate? They would have had to equip the cafeteria with oxygen masks. These guys had to eat to win and, believe me, they ate four to five times more than the average person.

As far as grades and classes went, there was no preferential treatment. If a practice conflicted with a class, we had to go to class. If you had a C or below in a course, you usually went to a tutor. If the tutor could take you only during practice, you would go to the tutor. If you didn't show, he'd come looking for you.

There were some teachers who took it easy on me because I was a football player. But it never affected how they graded me. They might not bother me if I didn't show up for a class, but that's as far as it went; I still had to do the work. If I didn't, Mr. DeCicco would get a call, and that always meant big trouble. There were also many professors who would go out of their way to give football players a hard time. A priest who taught my European history class was especially hard. I wanted to get out of the class because he was tough on everybody. I was just waiting for something to happen. One day, he was giving an unusually boring lecture, in one of those big semicircle-type lecture halls.

He was talking, and out of the corner of his eye he caught a student, who was in Navy ROTC and wearing his uniform, sleeping.

"Hey, you," the priest screamed. "Hey, Navy man." The guy jerked up so fast he fell out of his chair onto the floor and his little Navy hat went flying. "If you ever fall asleep in my class again I'll have you out of this school so fast your head will be spinning." The next day I was in Mr. DeCicco's office begging to get out of European history. Fortunately, he switched me.

Mr. DeCicco had a lot to do with helping me get out of school with a degree. He understood when I needed to change a class. But as understanding as he was, he was also forceful. Accounting was a problem for me. It was required in my major but I always felt I could get by without it. I was trying to convey that feeling to DeCicco. "Damn it, Joe, you at least have to get a C," he yelled. "I'll do everything I can to help. I know you don't like accounting and maybe you can't even handle it. But you're in this class, so grow up and work."

At least he was taking an interest. On the football field no one cared about how I was performing, but somehow, some way, I sustained myself. The key was that I've always believed I could walk onto a football field and make things happen. No matter how many people said I couldn't, I knew I could. Freshmen were not eligible to play on the varsity team when I entered Notre Dame. We had a few freshman games but I didn't get to play much. What the coaches would do was start one guy and let him play until he made a series of mistakes. I was pretty low on the totem pole, and by the time they reached me I only got to play a couple of minutes. Psychologically, things were really tough for me. I never sat on the bench, but worse than that, we had to go to the varsity games. I had to walk into a stadium full of people and couldn't even dress for the game. A few weeks of doing that was enough for me. I walked out of one game and began to cry.

Sometimes I wonder how I kept my confidence that year. It

was my friends who helped me through this period, a bunch of guys who later would become known as the Average White Backs (AWBs). When they ask where Montana got his inspiration—"Joe, was it George Gipp?" "Joe, was it Ara?" "Joe, was it the Golden Dome?" No, it was the Average White Backs. From left to right, big, bad, Steve Orsini—now the Dallas Cowboys' ticket manager—a gent who goes way back with me. We played together in "The Big 33 Game," a high school all-star game between Ohio and Pennsylvania. Then there were Terry Eurick and Steve Schmitz. Of course there was Mark Ewald and Nick DeCicco. They gave me so much strength, and we had so much fun. We did some crazy things. One was a scam Nick and I pulled our freshman year.

There was this guy Jimmy, from Pittsburgh, who had the soda concession and was proud of it. "Nick, this guy has a monopoly," I said.

"Let's break the sucker," Nick suggested.

Although our window looked out over the lobby area, it was positioned at the corner of the dorm so we also could get a good look over in the back, where they threw out the garbage. Jimmy kept his soda on the roof in the back of the dorm to keep it ice-cold. His dorm was right across from the chapel and just a short jump across a roof from our room. We went to the store and bought six-packs of warm pop at a bargain price. We would come back to the dorm, wait until the sun went down, jump across the roof, and replace his "expensive" cold soda with our warm supply. We were basically getting free soda. Sleazy, you say? Well, maybe, but it sure kept him on his toes. And I guess he gave two bored freshmen something to do.

Even with all these good people around me it was hard to ignore football at Notre Dame. The only feeling comparable to the emotion I felt before a Super Bowl was football Saturday in South Bend.

Most of my motivation comes from within me. I never really needed any coach's speech to get psyched to go out and play football. The game has always been so challenging to me that it has stood alone as my motivation to stay with the sport as long as I have. But when I looked around that locker room at Notre Dame, saw the "Win one for the Gipper" speech inscribed on the wall, well, even a cynic like me got chills. And then a funny thing happened on the way to spring practice. Ara resigned for personal and health reasons.

Don't let anyone who was around during that time tell you any different. Players were upset when Ara left, but they also had mixed reactions, because every position was thrown up for grabs. It would have been great to play for Ara but I wasn't going to get sentimental about that. The key to being successful in football is playing, no two ways about it.

When Dan Devine became the coach at Notre Dame, we all felt we had a better chance. We all believed that a new regime would be looking at new players to get the job done. Of course, the players who believed they were destined for a starting spot under Ara were unhappy. Devine upset some people. He wasn't one who looked for an orderly transition. He took control and began aggressively force-feeding his system to young men who thought Ara was a living legend. But in reality, no matter who the coach is, everyone wants to start. I liked Ara but I figured I had a better chance of starting under Devine.

I couldn't care less what Devine was doing. The new coach only added to my feeling that I should be playing. If an athlete says, "Hey, that guy's great, he's better than me," well, the guy is in big trouble. Once you start thinking that people are better than you, you start giving up. That's when you are destined to stay on the bottom. Sometimes I look back and wonder where all my mental toughness came from. I've seen guys who seemed to be ten times stronger than me but I always thought I was better.

During spring practice I was doing everything right. For the first time that year I felt good about football. In the annual Blue and Gold spring game I played well. I figured that next year I would have a shot at being the starting quarterback. Rick Slager, watch out; Montana is right on your heels.

In the beginning of my sophomore year, I got a good look at how Dan Devine was going to coach. I felt he was wishy-washy. He would never stick to one quarterback. Slager played in the first two games against Boston College and Purdue. The offense really didn't play that well against the Boilermakers. Next up was Northwestern.

We were losing 7–0 in the first quarter and Slager hit an 11-yard pass to Mark McLane, taking us down to the Northwestern 49-yard line. On the next play he ran an option on the left side and gained 4 yards before he was hammered. He had that drunken look, and I knew he had been hurt.

Finally, it would be my turn. I completed the drive with halfback Al Hunter scoring from the 2. I remember trying to call an audible. I called it one way, then another. I was confused and so was everyone else, but the nervousness left when I realized Devine was going to leave me in the game.

My next series began after Willie Fry blocked a punt and Tom Lopienski covered it at the Northwestern 26. We scored four plays later when our fullback Jim Browner went 12 yards on a pitch play.

My confidence was building when I saw how our offense could easily control the Wildcats' defensive line. On our next possession we went 70 yards on six plays, including my first touchdown pass, a 14-yard pass over the middle to McLane. The day ended with me scoring a touchdown in the fourth quarter. We had a fourth and goal from Northwestern's 6. I faked a pitch, got a great block from Jim Weiler, a reserve halfback, and scored. It was 31–7 and I finally had contributed to a Notre Dame win.

Looking back on that game, I probably would have been more nervous if Devine had started me—fat chance of that happening. My father came into the locker room after the game to congratulate me. The reporters wanted to find out how he felt after his son's first win. The sportswriters converged on him and they were all over me. It was a strange but exciting experience. This euphoria lasted for about a day. When we reported back to practice, I found out that I still wasn't the starter. I was really upset; considering my performance in the Northwestern game, what more could I do?

I was beginning to think that doing something miraculous was the only way I could get Devine to play me. Or should I say, a miracle performance would put pressure on him to start me. Two weeks later, the opportunity would present itself. We were in Chapel Hill, playing the University of North Carolina. Rick couldn't get anything going in the first half, and Carolina couldn't mount any offense either. The half ended in a scoreless tie.

Naturally, I thought Devine should have let me start the second half, but he had other ideas. We went into the fourth quarter trailing 14–0. Then Rick took us on a 65-yard drive in twelve plays. He tried to hit tight end Ken MacAfee for the 2-point conversion, but that failed. The next time we got the ball, Slager had three consecutive incomplete passes. Now Devine tells me to get ready. Shit, talk about being put on the spot! Carolina was pumped and it was over 90 degrees on the field. We had the ball on our own 27-yard line and started to drive. We went the distance on five plays. Jerome Heavens blasted up the middle for 20 yards; I hit on a sideline pass good for 7, and then hit Dan Kelleher for 39 yards, moving us to their 2-yard line. Al Hunter took it in, making it 14–12. They shot everyone at me to try to stop the 2-point conversion, but I eluded the rush and hit Doug Buth to tie the game.

Carolina moved the ball well down to our 26-yard line but missed a field goal with 1:15 left.

The next series of plays really combined all the elements necessary to a winning quarterback: reading a defense, trusting one's instincts, getting the ball to the receiver, and a hell of a lot of luck. With 1:03 left we had a second and 10 from our own 20. Devine called a draw play, but as I lined up I saw their cornerback, Russ Conley, playing deep.

"Ninety-one, ninety-one," I shouted.

That audible is a quick turnout or sideline pass designed to pick up about 8 yards. I dropped back and hit Ted Burgmeier on the sideline. Conley came up on the ball, trying to intercept the pass. He slipped, and Teddy ran 80 yards to give us the win. Things were timed perfectly. If Conley hadn't slipped or if I'd thrown the ball late I might have watched him taking the ball back the other way. That's what they call luck. This game really made the powers that be turn on the Notre Dame nostalgia. I remember Moose Krause, our athletic director, addressing the troops after the win. "I've been around since the days of Knute Rockne and I'm telling you this was the greatest comeback by a Notre Dame team I've ever seen," he said. "It was hot and humid, I know several of you were hurt. But you all hung in there. I'm extremely proud of all of you."

And Devine: "This was my best victory ever. More satisfying than anything that happened at Arizona State or Missouri or Green Bay."

As for me, well, I was excited but I didn't go overboard. I knew my fate was calculated on a week-to-week basis. But don't think I was blasé about that win; to pull off something like that under the Notre Dame microscope felt terrific. The next week was the University of Southern California. As things turned out, each of my three games with USC would be memorable, this one for what *didn't* happen.

There was no way that Devine could keep me on the bench. We got off to a flying start. On the second play of the game, I handed to Al Hunter and he went 52 yards to put us ahead. We missed the extra point but had an early 6–0 lead. The early scoring didn't bother USC. It didn't help that I wasn't moving the team. Our defense was playing great. They gave me the ball in USC territory a couple of times during the first half and we couldn't put it in.

They took things into their own hands near the end of the half. Luther Bradley blocked a punt and Tom Lopienski picked it up at the 3 and ran it in. A penalty nullified the score but we got an instant replay. Bradley blocked the punt again and Lopienski recovered it again and scored. We scored on the 2-point conversion when Hunter threw an option pass to Kris Haines to give us a 14-7 lead at the half. (The Trojans had scored their touchdown in the second quarter, when Vince Evans hit Shelton Diggs with a 21-yard scoring pass.) The offense stank in the first half. Incredibly, we were winners, but USC had controlled the ball 21:49 of the first half.

Things were just as bad in the second half, and USC took advantage this time. On the third play of the third quarter I tried to hit Haines, but Jim Hovan intercepted the pass, giving them the ball at our 37. Ricky Bell and Mosi Tatupu took control, taking turns running it down to our 3 before Bell scored, tying the game. Late in the third quarter we went on a drive led by AWB Steve Orsini. The drive ended in a field goal. Going into the fourth quarter, we led by 3. But Bell and Tatupu seemed to be unstoppable. They took turns running from their 25-yard line into our end zone, putting them ahead by 4 points, 21-17. There would be no "miracles" on this day. When we got the ball back I threw an interception, which resulted in a USC field goal. We got the ball back one more time but didn't move it. Ricky Bell devastated us, carrying the ball forty times for 165 yards.

Except for a 31-30 comeback win against Air Force—we were down 30-7 at the half—I didn't play much the rest of the season. Little did I know that I wouldn't get into a game that meant anything for about two years. Although I had been given a chance, I still had a problem with not playing much. I'm no fun to be around when I'm benched.

Even if I feel lousy, if the coach wants me to play and I can still walk, I will play. A game during the 1985 season was a good example. The night before a 49er game against the Lions I had the flu and felt terrible. I was tossing and turning all night, I had diarrhea, and my muscles ached. When we arrived at the Silverdome in Pontiac, I felt like hammered crap. They hooked me to an IV and pumped me full of a solution to replace the fluids that I'd lost during the night. Somehow I played that game, and when Bill took me out right before our final possession, hell, I was upset but I understood. I had no strength left. So you see, I don't like sitting on the bench.

When I came back for my junior year, Slager was gone and I figured I'd be the starting quarterback. I figured wrong. Devine didn't name me as a starter, and once again I had to battle it out for my position. This was to be one of the worst years of my life.

We were going into the last scrimmage before the season started and practice was just about over. Devine came down out of the tower. "Keep working on getting the ball in from the ten," he ordered. Hell, we had been busting it in over and over again from in close for about half an hour and he wanted to keep on. But he was the boss. In the huddle I called a play action pass. I made the fake to the halfback and slipped and started going down. Out of the corner of my eye I saw Willie Fry charging toward me. No one blocked him.

The first rule in taking a hard sack is to avoid the initial blow. I'll make a quick move so a defender doesn't get a clean shot. Actually, it's sometimes better if you don't see the defender coming because your body is already relaxed. Now I thought slipping had saved me from a vicious hit, because I was loose and going down before Willie got to me. I fell on my shoulder and Willie was on top of me as I went down; his six-foot, four-inch, 240-pound body bounced on me, separating my shoulder.

That ended the 1976 season before it even started. Well, it almost ended. I learned something about how Devine operated. The coaches told me if I could suit up for practice with four games left they would let me travel with the team. Even though I knew I wasn't going to play that year, with six games left to play, I came back and began practicing. They did me a big favor; they let me dress for one home game. That season was frustrating, but I learned not to take anything for granted. Traveling with the team might seem trivial, but what was important was the knowledge at that point in my career that I really couldn't trust Dan Devine.

My Chance

When Tom Parise wheeled a cafeteria-tray cart through our meeting room, which was the cafeteria, I wondered what was going to happen. Parise was the team actor. He could imitate everybody. We had talent shows at the end of each season and Tom was always the master of ceremonies. He could do a great Ara impression and Muhammad Ali too.

He also was a hell of a fullback. When I was a freshman he played behind Wayne Bullock. A pretty good fullback, Bullock graduated that year, and everyone expected Tom to move in. Devine probably did too until that day Tom performed on the cart in the meeting room. Tom didn't care who he picked on and everyone accepted his teasing as good-natured kidding. I guess Devine didn't.

The cart was in the middle of the cafeteria, and Tom hopped on it. It was our annual freshman talent show and Tom started doing an imitation of Devine in the coaching tower. Dan walked in in the middle of this routine. He didn't say anything but the look on his face told it all. Tom didn't start the following year. I don't think Dan Devine liked to be teased.

My opinion of Devine changed after I had been away from Notre Dame a few years and made an effort to put things in perspective. When I was playing I felt he took credit for everything. I think any coach who is having success tries to make people think that it's his coaching that has made a winner. Now I can understand that. When I was at Notre Dame I couldn't. All I wanted, when I came back from my injury, was a chance. Maybe I wasn't playing that well but at least I wanted to play to prove that I wasn't so terrible.

The mistake I made when I wasn't playing was letting people know I was angry about it. At that point I learned one of life's great lessons: Often it's the people who can b.s. the best, the politicians, the phonies, who get ahead, and nobody likes a complainer. Things seemed to be taking the same old frustrating course when I came back for the 1977 season, my junior year. I was the third-string quarterback behind Rusty Lisch and Gary Forystek. It took a series of very unusual events to give me a shot at the job against Purdue in the third game of the season. My chance to play didn't come because of anything I did on the field. Rather, it arrived out of necessity. We were on our way to losing the game. We had a 1-1 record going into the game. Devine started Lisch and he played most of the first half. In the second half I was still on the bench. He put Gary Forystek in the game and Fred Arrington hit him hard. Gary was knocked out, suffering a broken neck and clavicle, the worst injury I've ever seen on a field. They couldn't move him for a while and things looked very bad. I was sure I would be going into the game but Devine decided to come back with Lisch.

At that moment I felt totally beaten. If I ever thought sincerely about quitting football it was then. That feeling turned to anger and disgust, and I began cursing on the sidelines. I wasn't talking to anyone in particular—I just hoped one of the coaches would hear me. I didn't know if Devine heard me or not and I didn't care.

This pattern of my having to prove myself went back to high school, where I also thought that I was better than the guy who was playing ahead of me. That was Paul Timko, who was built more like a tight end than a quarterback. During my sophomore year we played back and forth, but midway through the season they switched him to defensive end. Sure, I was happy, but I paid for it. He wore me out in practice. He kicked my ass up and down the field until they moved him to tight end. Then he sure changed his tune. He became Mr. Nice Guy because he wanted something from me—the football. I got the ball to him. This big guy had to be kept happy.

So here I was, years later, in the Purdue game, with just under two minutes left in the third quarter. We were trailing 24–14. Devine had played his other two quarterbacks right down to the end and we still were behind. He called for me to go into the game. Again he was placing me in a difficult spot but in my mood I didn't care about the situation, I was going in there to go for broke. Tight end Ken MacAfee and a few of the others reminded me about the comebacks we had made before. They wanted me to believe in myself and I appreciated that. I bobbled the first snap and then threw a wobbly incompletion to MacAfee.

"OK, the butterflies are gone, let's win this thing," I said. I had to tell them something to let them know I wasn't losing it. We drove into field-goal range and Dave Reeve hit a 24-yarder to move us a little bit closer. We got the ball back quickly on a Luther Bradley interception. I hit MacAfee with a 13-yard touchdown pass and suddenly the score was tied. With 4:12 left in the game we started a drive at our own 42 and got down the field on passes to Haines and MacAfee, before David Mitchell, a sophomore back, scored the winning touchdown with 1:39 left in the game. Some people say this gave us the shot we needed to win the national championship that year.

I won the quarterback job that day. When I look back at it, I still have mixed feelings about the way the whole thing was handled. Sometimes I think it came down to luck, and the fact that two quarterbacks were hurt—not my ability. We went undefeated the rest of the year. But the thing that still sticks out about that championship season was the USC game.

Devine was aware what USC had done to us the previous year. This was a traditional and bitter rivalry, and everyone was looking for an edge. A group of students had built a Trojan horse and asked Devine if the captains of the team could hide inside it and be wheeled onto the field for the coin toss. He wouldn't buy that idea. He had his own idea to psych us. Months before the game he'd ordered green jerseys for the game. Notre Dame had not worn the green since Thanksgiving Day, 1963. All week long the battle cry on campus was Think green, wear green. People were writing odes to the color green, and at the pep rally the night before the game, Digger Phelps, the basketball coach, got into the act and so did Devine, again just talking green and the Irish tradition.

When we came out for our warmups we were wearing our normal blue-and-gold game jerseys but we had on green socks. The crowd was chanting, "Green machine, green machine." We began feeling the emotion but no one knew why we had the green socks on and no one really cared. When we came into the locker room after the warmups everyone had new green jerseys hanging in their lockers. The big guys, the linemen, went berserk. They started beating on each other, butting helmets. It was scary. Little things can give you a lift before a game and this had a terrific effect on us. The crowd went nuts when we came out on the field wearing green. The green dream came true.

We blew USC away 49–12.

The rest of the season was almost anticlimactic. Notre Dame was getting a lot of national attention that year because we were driving for the championship. The pressure wasn't as intense as it is in the pros, but it taught me a lesson about what the national spotlight could be like.

It forced me to grow up pretty fast, even though I wasn't ready. People take it for granted that you can mature like anyone else when you are playing football. That's not true. Just surviving doesn't always mean you come out without some scars, some bittersweet memories, and some damn hard lessons.

When I entered Notre Dame my goal was getting a degree

and a good education. Mom and Dad sacrificed a lot for me to get to college. They knew what it was like making every paycheck count and I knew the meaning of living within the restrictions of a tight budget. Pro football was my dream, but I knew that in my case making it in the pros was by no means a sure thing. I didn't take school lightly.

Academically, Notre Dame was tough for me. During my sophomore year I was on academic probation. Trying to get my grades up while also trying to become the starting quarterback wasn't conducive to concentrating on either studies or football. When my grades went down, I tended to bulk up on the books rather than studying game film. I sacrificed one for the other and hoped for the best. I didn't know this at the time, but I was growing through experience. I had come a long way. The loneliness of being away from home, the realization that Devine thought I was at my best on the bench, and facing an academic regimen that tested me as I'd never been tested before, was a lot to handle.

I was also experiencing another strange feeling. It was hard for me to go home. This was strange because my family always provided me with the love and inspiration I needed to carry on. But once I had been away from Monongahela, and started a life of my own, I didn't want to go back. My problems were probably no different from those of the other freshman football players, but the DeCiccos were always there for me, whether I asked for help or not. When I decided to get married during my second semester of freshman year to Kim, the girl I'd dated in high school, they said I should wait.

That was hard on Mom and Dad because they wanted me to come home. When I did go back I felt like I was taking a step backward, like I was stifling my new life. I didn't realize I was hurting them. Later in life I learned you may outgrow your hometown but you never outgrow your family.

But what did I know? I was on my way to the Cotton Bowl.

4

Welcome to Dallas

Dallas.

This kid from western Pennsylvania really had no idea that his life was going to be linked to this city of Stetsons, cheerleaders, and barbecue. I hated Dallas for a stupid reason. My cousin Michael was a big Dallas Cowboys fan. That's all he ever talked about when we talked football as kids. It didn't leave me with a good feeling for the Cowboys or the city. But my first trip to Big D would be the easiest.

Of course, at the time I didn't know that. The odds were stacked against Notre Dame. Our opponent, the University of Texas, was ranked number one in the country and had a few other things going for them. They were playing at home, they had the Heisman Trophy winner Earl Campbell, the Outland Trophy winner Brad Shearer, and a whole lot of confidence. I was kind of relieved to be away from Notre Dame. Kim and I had had an amenable parting of the ways and the pressures of that break, school, and football were closing in on me.

Texas made a stupid mistake during the week prior to the game. Shearer called Ernie Hughes, one of our guards, and Ken

MacAfee, our tight end, "average" blockers. These two guys got real fired up and their anger was contagious. It helped all of us. Both our offensive and defensive lines dominated Texas. Saying they kicked Texas butts all over the field is an understatement. They owned the trenches. They might as well have been playing a high school team. We won 38–10 and it was never close. Campbell ran for 116 yards on twenty-nine carries, but his longest run of the day was for only 18 yards.

Both of our big backs went for over 100. Jerome Heavens had 102 and Vegas Ferguson gained 100. Our preparation was centered on seven or eight running plays. We went ahead 24–10 in the first half and shut them out 14–0 in the second half. Terry Eurick scored two touchdowns for us and Vegas had three, one on a 17-yard pass from me. Winning the national championship in the Cotton Bowl that year was memorable, but when I think about the state of Texas and the Cotton Bowl, the game that stands out is the Cotton Bowl against Houston in '79, my final game for Notre Dame.

That was probably the most bizarre game I ever played. The first thing was the weather. The frosty winters of western Pennsylvania were familiar to me, but I never thought they could make their way down South. I always thought Dallas was a warm-weather city. It was chilly when we played Texas in '78, but in '79 we might as well have been playing Houston in Green Bay, Wisconsin.

The week of the game I came down with the flu. When I pulled the covers over my head the night before the game I fell asleep to the sound of ice pelting the hotel window. When I got up the next morning and looked out the hotel window, it was beautiful, beautiful if you were spending the day indoors looking out a window. The city looked like a petrified forest. The ice coated the trees and was hanging off everything.

This was a day to watch football from the comfort of your living room, not a day to play it.

When we arrived at the stadium and went out to walk on the field, there was at least an inch of ice covering the artificial turf. The stadium maintenance guys were scraping it off as best they could. The harder parts were being covered with rock salt. Hell, I wondered how it was going to feel falling on that carpet. Maybe like bouncing off a frozen porcupine! The wind was gusting at thirty miles per hour, making the temperature feel like 10 below zero. This was the Cotton Bowl, my farewell to Notre Dame. But I didn't care much about the game during the first half. Neither did anyone else.

It all started with the opening kickoff. We won the toss and elected to take field position. We took the side where the hawk, Mr. Wind, was blowing behind our back. Houston countered by electing to kick off. Did you ever know anyone who sat and looked at you like they sincerely understood what you were saying when, in reality, their mind was somewhere in deep left center field? Well that's where everyone's head was during the coin toss. Our kickoff team runs onto the field. Their kickoff team runs onto the field. Two kickers face off. Two kicking tees are on the field. I mean, to quote Casey Stengel: Can anyone here play this game?

About 39,500 people who purchased tickets to the game played it smart and stayed home. The players all would have rather been curled up in front of a fireplace; the hell with the game, let's just keep our butts warm. When someone came off the field he hustled over to the blowers by the bench. If it wasn't so cold Devine probably would have done what he always did when he was a little nervous—patted that bald spot on the back of his head.

Taking the wind was a smart move because it helped us jump off to a quick 12–0 lead. Houston running back Emmett King fumbled after Houston moved to our 36. We drove 66 yards for the first score of the game. I scored the first touchdown on a 3-yard run, but the key play was a screen pass to Heavens that went for 27 yards. We scored a few minutes later after recovering another fumble, which our linebacker Bob Crable picked up at the Houston 25. We missed an extra point on both scores but we had our 12–0 lead. Both defenses played semiwell, but everything was going Houston's way. Every time something happened near their bench they would be laughing at us, telling us how they were going to win. They had reason to pop off. After our scores, they ran up 20 points.

All the scoring was done at one end of the stadium because the wind was blowing so hard at the other we felt like we were playing against a hurricane. It was almost impossible to feel the ball through our frostbitten fingers. At the half I arrived in the locker room shaking uncontrollably. My temperature had dropped to 96 degrees. This was really strange; I couldn't control my body. The doctor and trainers covered me with blankets and coats. I began drinking as much chicken soup as I could. As my body warmed, that feeling I had had earlier—not wanting to play because of the cold—disappeared. I wanted to go back and take another shot.

Timmy Koegel came in for me at quarterback, and with about 4:40 left in the third quarter we were trailing 34–12. Although I'm not Mr. Rah-Rah, I didn't want my last game at Notre Dame to end after the first half. Late in the third quarter I was ready to come back. The mind can conquer all. It was just as cold, just as nasty, and I had no feeling in my hands when I returned to the field. But now I wanted in. I figured we still had a good shot even though we were far behind. Once I got back on the field I didn't consider my health. The only thing I really thought about was being able to play without getting those shakes again. Even a sack would probably be better than that feeling.

The first series was bad. We went 7 yards to our own 27-yard line before I threw an interception, my third of the day. Fortunately, in the fourth quarter we had the wind at our back, and got great field position each time we got the ball. With 7:37 left in the game the play that I think turned the game around took place. Houston had a fourth down and needed 6 for the first. They lined up to punt and Tony Belden, a freshman reserve fullback, broke through and blocked Jay Wyatt's punt. The ball popped up straight in the air and another freshman,

Steve Cichy, outjumped everyone, picked the ball out of the air, and ran it in for the score. I hit Vegas in the corner of the end zone, cutting the lead to 34–20. As far as I was concerned, we were back in business. Our defense held Houston on their next possession and we took over at our own 39-yard line with 5:40 left. I hit Dean Masztak with a 17-yard pass and came right back to hit Heavens with a pass good for 30 yards. The next play was a big one. I threw downfield for Pete Holohan at the Houston 3. The pass was incomplete but Gerald Cook, one of their DBs, was called for interference. Three plays later I scored on a 2-yard run. We had just gone 61 yards in 1:22. I hit Kris Haines for the 2-point conversion. It was 34–28.

Things were definitely getting interesting. Our defense held Houston, and we got the ball on the Houston 49-yard line with 2:25 left in the game. We moved to their 36, and on a first-down play I almost cost us the game. I dropped back to pass and couldn't find anyone. This was no time to think too much, so I pulled the ball down and took off straight up the middle. The defense was stunned as I cruised down to the 20, but David Hodge ripped the ball out of my arms. Houston recovered the ball at their 20 with 2:05 left in the game. Things looked real bleak. The defense held Houston, and with a fourth and 6 from their 24 with forty-six seconds left in the game, Houston got set to punt. We called time-out.

I haven't played in many games where a penalty against my team helped save a game, but this was one of them. Our defense put a strong rush on Jay Wyatt and he got off a 21-yard punt. Because the defense went all out to block the punt, they were caught off side. Houston coach Bill Yeoman decided to accept the penalty, setting up a fourth and 1 at their own 29 with thirty-five seconds left in the game. Houston quarterback Danny Davis turned to hand off to Emmett King. King moved to the ball too fast and brushed Davis. The handoff was clean but he was slowed up enough to be caught by Joe Gramke, our right defensive end. The ball was ours with twenty-eight seconds left. I took off on the first play and gained 11 yards. Then

Haines shook free and I hit him at the Houston 8-yard line. Houston called time-out to reset their defense with six seconds left in the game.

In the huddle I called an out pattern to Kris Haines. I took a quick two-step drop and released the ball quickly. He was wide open but my pass was low and away. That stopped the clock with two seconds left in the game.

I came back to the sidelines to confer with Devine, I wasn't thinking about missing the pass; I was thinking about practice that week. We all thought Dan was nuts. He kept making us run that play, the 91 out pass, over and over again. It brought back memories of that inside-the-10 drill when Willie Fry nailed me and put me out for the entire 1976 season. Dan just had me throw the ball low and outside in the corner over and over again, making the receivers dive, and believe me, they were pissed off. As I came to the sidelines to discuss the last play of my college career, there was no doubt in my mind what play to call. For once everything made sense. "Joe, one shot, what do you think?" Devine asked.

"I like the same play again."

"Run it again," he said.

If we were in a sports movie this would be the cliché slow-motion shot the director would use. I'll speed it up for you. I rolled right and threw the same low outside pass in the right corner of the end zone. Kris dove, caught the ball in bounds, and rolled out of bounds.

The score was now 34–34, there was no time left in the game, and we weren't out of the woods yet. Joe Unis, our backup placekicker, who had grown up in Dallas, had to kick the winning point. He knocked it through, but an illegal procedure penalty nullified. He stepped up and did it again, giving us the 35–34 win in a truly weird game.

My college career was over. Devine had actually asked me what to do, what I thought would work. After five years of uncertainty and coaches calling plays for me, I had gotten to make the final decision.

When the reporters asked Devine about the last call, he gave me the credit. He could have taken the credit and I wouldn't have said a thing, but he gave it to me. He also demonstrated his confidence in me when someone asked him why he'd stuck with me when I was having a poor first half. (Unfortunately, all this support came following my final game.) "I'm a one-quarterback coach and I always have been," Devine said. "Joe is my quarterback and he stays in the game unless things become so desperate that I feel a change would be in the team's best interest." Well, I couldn't pay much attention to the talk. It was such a great win for us there was no use trying to figure out Devine's motives.

Reporters were asking me if I realized that we had just played in a classic football game. Yeah, maybe we did, but other things were running through my mind. It was a time for reflection. During the last three years at Notre Dame, Devine had really done nothing to boost my confidence. In fact, he had never given me much credit until now. Why couldn't he have been easier? Why couldn't he have been more open? Why do coaches play games with people's minds? I guess I'll never know because I never went back and talked to him about it.

Maybe I learned a lesson. It is part of my nature to give someone the benefit of the doubt, to think they mean well. My stay at Notre Dame changed my attitude. Devine never let me know what he was up to. Believe me, after that Houston game, my conversion from a believer to a skeptic was complete.

But sitting in that locker room, in the middle of a great celebration, it occurred to me that no coach wants to give you credit while you are playing for him. Maybe Devine was playing mind games with me, but maybe it was strategy. He had the ability to keep me on edge, keep me on my toes.

My years at Notre Dame were filled with doubt and frustration. But in the end, things worked out. Maybe Devine even prepared me for what was about to come. As my Notre Dame career was coming to a close, things seemed to be running pretty smoothly for me. But that was only on the surface. In reality, I was still up against it. I had to settle a divorce. I realized that Kim and I had rushed into our marriage; I guess we needed each other. In reality, we had different perspectives on life. We were growing up in different ways.

But things weren't super serious as my college career was coming to a close. I moved into a place off campus with my cousin Michael. We lived in an apartment over a bar and there was a lot of partying going on in all the units. One time I went to do some night skiing near South Bend. It had started to snow on the way back so when I got home I just parked my car, took my skis off the rack, and headed for my apartment. Fortunately, I didn't have classes for the next few days, so Mike and I got a lot of pizza and beer and stayed up pretty late just shooting the bull. The next morning it was still snowing—a real Midwestern blizzard. Some cars were starting to get out the third day, but mine was buried. We rented the place from Joe Serge, a South Bend city councilman, but he said he thought there was nothing he could do. "Joe, I'll check into it tomorrow and see what I can come up with," he said.

The next night there was a real loud party going on and some guy from across the hall started banging on my door. Well, I was feeling a little cooped up and really wasn't ready for some drunk who wanted to stick his fist through the door. Fortunately, I cooled out and listened to what he had to say.

"Montana, if you want your damn car towed there's a tank outside that will do it." Booze does strange things to people.

"What the hell have you been drinking?" I asked this guy. When I went outside there was a big old mean monster tank right in front of our apartment. About five National Guardsmen were hanging on the tank. All five were chugging beer.

"Hey, boy, we'll tow your car but we won't be responsible for ripping the shit out of your front bumper." I just wanted the car out, with or without a front bumper. The guardsman on top of the tank must have been in another world. He did a pretty fair swan dive from the top of the tank into the snow near my front bumper. He started digging under my front bumper like a dog searching for a bone. They pulled my car out with no problem.

That incident was probably one time things went smoothly for me at Notre Dame. I liked playing there and enjoyed being part of the tradition, but it was a relief to finally get away from the Golden Dome. When I look back at periods of my life I usually translate them into school years. You're the best athlete in the sixth grade, then all of a sudden you're in junior high school and you have to start from the bottom all over again. The pattern goes on for a football player until he hits the pros. There you may start as low man but if you make it, there's no looking back. Now I was going to be able to concentrate on one thing— football. I didn't have to worry about grades and going to class.

I had done my time. I was ready.

Taking Care of Business

I wasn't deluged by agents while I was at Notre Dame. A few came to talk to me. Larry Muno, the gentleman I eventually signed with, was one; Mike Trope, a Southern Californian with a reputation for delivering big contracts, contacted me, as did a company known as Professional Athletes Management Company (PAMCO). When I graduated in December—I graduated late because I had an extra year of football eligibility resulting from my shoulder injury in 1976—I headed for Los Angeles. I wanted to set up shop in a warm climate away from the cold weather. I had had enough of the windchill factor.

I decided to sign with PAMCO. I really needed some financial help. They didn't give me any money but they arranged and co-signed a $7,500 bank loan. There was no way I was going to ask my parents for the cash, so I handled it the best I could. But there was something I didn't like about PAMCO. The principals in the company didn't seem to have a heck of a lot of experience with football players. I was working out where the Rams practice, and Dick Steinberg, who was then player personnel director of the Rams, asked me if I had an agent. I hemmed and hawed, finally telling him that I was "kind of" with PAMCO. But I asked Dick if he knew anyone else. He recommended Larry.

There was a connection between Larry and me. Not only had Larry Muno come up to talk to me at Notre Dame, but his son Kevin was a punter for the Irish, who, as a sophomore, was called on to punt in his first varsity game, that key win against Purdue in 1977. Kevin came through in the clutch, averaging 36 yards on six kicks, including a couple of boomers that left Purdue deep in their own territory. I called Larry and met with him. We talked about my situation but he never mentioned representing me. I sensed he knew something was troubling me. "I don't know what it is," I said. "But something about these guys bothers me." Larry, who heads an organization of agents called the Association of Representatives of Professional Athletes— known as ARPA—and who has extensive connections on the West Coast, told me he would check PAMCO out. "I appreciate it," I said. "But I want to tell you, I'm also talking to Mike Trope about representing me." He told me that he would check them out anyway.

Trope had apparently been trying to make some inroads at Notre Dame. He had competed with Larry for Steve Heimkreiter. When I went up to his home he really pitched me hard. Larry had told me that Trope said he would do Heimkreiter's contract for free. Trope offered to do my contract for an extremely nominal fee. It was obvious to me that Mike desperately wanted to represent a Notre Dame guy. Maybe it was in my own head but I got bad vibes from Mike. He alluded to places I should go and be seen in, which is not my style. After that meeting with Trope I also saw Larry. My meetings with Larry caused me to do some soul searching. I wanted to be decisive. Although I had signed with PAMCO, I knew that it wasn't in my best interests. I came back to Larry and asked him to represent me. "What do I have to do to untangle this mess?" I asked.

"The first thing you've got to do is send them a recision letter," he said. "You also probably will have to pay them back some money."

I sent them the letter and came on strong. I told them I didn't feel they could represent me in a manner that would be beneficial to me. The tone of my letter suggested that they really didn't know what they were doing when it came to football. They got back to me and, to my surprise, agreed that there should be an amicable parting of the ways.

Manhattan Beach is a beautiful little spot in Southern California. It's beaches, boats, and volleyball. The shops along the main street are those little ones that give the whole place the feeling of a small tourist town. After five years at Notre Dame and the cold Midwestern winters I really wanted to play in a warm-weather city. I had arranged to buy a little place where I could look out the window and see the beach. Subconsciously, I guess I felt that if my residence was on the beach maybe I would be drafted by one of the West Coast teams.

In reality, I wasn't going to be picky. The idea was to play in the NFL; that's what I had to prepare myself for and that's what I wanted to do. Although I think I have an aptitude for the design area of advertising, I wasn't looking at that as a career path, at least not now. This was a very strange period. I had to prepare for playing for team X. It's kind of funny—you don't know what's in store but you try to work out as best you can. I attended workouts where scouts congregate to watch potential draft picks. I went to a big one in New York. I also showed my stuff in workouts for the Packers, Rams, and 49ers.

Now maybe you've heard that old story about the Hollywood agent with a big cigar in his mouth who walks up to a novice actor, puffs on his smoke, takes the cigar out of his mouth, and pokes the dude with it. "Stick with me, kid, I'm gonna make you a star." Believe me, this was not too different from what I was going through in 1979. Scouts would come up to me and tell me that they were going to take me in the first or second round. After this happened about six times I didn't know who to believe. They would look me in the eyes and tell me they were going to pick me as soon as they could. Because I graduated from school in December, I knew I would be living in this state of limbo until the draft in April.

A lot of stories have circulated about just how the 49ers became interested in me. Some say John Brodie, the former San Francisco quarterback, was instrumental in convincing Bill to draft me. I like to think I convinced Bill myself when he came down to Los Angeles to work out James Owens, a highly touted running back from UCLA. It seemed that I was there as an afterthought. I was in the area so they could kill two birds with one stone. In my mind their main interest was Owens.

Sam Wyche, the 49ers' quarterback coach at the time, was watching me. Most of the stuff we did was for the benefit of James, not me. But as the workout progressed, Sam started testing my arm to see if I could throw certain kinds of passes. Not only the short stuff but passes that you just drop over the linebackers, the touch-type things and the muscle passes.

If the 49ers weren't interested in me, Sam wouldn't have asked me to do such a wide variety of things. A few years later Sam told me that Bill was interested in me from the beginning; I wasn't a revelation to them that day on the practice field.

After all these workouts neither Larry nor I had any better idea what round I would go in. We "narrowed" it down to somewhere between the first and the fifth. How's that for going out on a limb?

On draft day Larry and I set up shop in the Kettle, a restaurant in Manhattan Beach. The only other time I would have this feeling was when awaiting the arrival of my daughter, Alexandra, in 1985. You sit and wait to hear when your number is called. Larry called his office every ten minutes to find out what was happening. Meanwhile, we kept pouring the coffee down until we got our answer: the San Francisco 49ers in the third round. I was the eighty-second pick in the draft. Bill had selected Owens in the second round.

A few things struck me as being positive. Bill picked me over Steve Dils, a quarterback he'd coached at Stanford. Having seen Dils play, he knew just how coachable he was, while he didn't know anything about me. Dils was still available when the 49ers picked me. I thought most people would have selected Dils before me because he had a more consistent record in college. Also, San Francisco was a team in transition, a team searching for an identity. This meant I would get a good shot at the quarterback job.

This, coupled with the Dils situation, really did a lot to boost my confidence, but the next few weeks were going to test it severely. Knowing the situation the 49ers were in, Larry and I felt we had some negotiating power, perhaps more than the normal second-round pick. They didn't have an established quarterback. Steve DeBerg was playing quarterback, and both Steve and Scott Bull, the backup, were coming off knee surgery. We just looked at what second-round picks were signing for, pricing them like refrigerators, and arrived at a number we thought best represented my value. We both felt that I should be the highest-paid player in my round. I felt that I was definitely a part of the 49ers' long-term plans; I figured that I was worth a certain price and was unwilling to budge.

The 49ers didn't see things my way.

I went to minicamp in Redwood City, the 49ers training facility, without a contract. One of the sticking points on the contract was a loan I wanted tied into my signing bonus. The Niners' signing bonus was also about $5,000 less than I wanted. And we were $8,000 apart on my yearly salary. The 49ers were one week away from the reporting date to the regular training camp, which was then at the University of Santa Clara, and we were still far apart on the numbers. That final week was quite interesting. My career as a Niner almost ended before I even reported to camp. John Ralston, who was the 49ers' vice-president for administration and the man who handled most of the contract negotiations, called Larry the Tuesday before we were supposed to report to training camp.

"We can't make a deal with you," he told Larry. "We're going to let you trade Joe for us. All we want is a number-three draft choice back."

"Thank you very much, John," Larry said nonchalantly. "I'll make a few calls and we'll get right back to you."

I was getting a fast education in the business of football. I was adamant about getting what I thought was top dollar immediately. Why? Because there is no such thing as free agency in pro football. The owners and the league seem to have this system—some would define it as collusion—that prevents anyone, and I mean anyone, from getting the kind of money people in baseball get when they play out their contract. Hey, if I didn't get top dollar going in, who knows what I would be worth when my contract expired?

Larry was calm because we had been tipped off by someone inside the 49er organization that Ralston was going to come at us with some new strategy. Larry called the Denver Broncos and the Chicago Bears, and both of them wanted me. As a matter of fact, Denver was willing to give me more money than I was asking from the 49ers. They were ready to trade Craig Penrose, a quarterback, and a draft pick for me. Larry had called Denver purposely because Ralston had worked there as a coach, and Larry knew having Denver call John might get under his skin.

Throughout the negotiations, the 49ers were doing their best to put pressure on me. In the newspapers Bill was saying our "demands" were exorbitant. Sam Wyche was in direct contact with me. His message was somewhat threatening and not what I really needed to hear at the time. "You're wrong to do this, Joe. Our offer is fair," he told me. "You're going to upset Bill and throw off any plans we have for getting you into our offensive system." I knew this was Sam's job. He had to put pressure on me. His mission was to make me feel guilty and he was doing a good job. Although I really wanted to get started, there was no way I was going to compromise.

The Thursday before training camp was scheduled to begin, I met with Larry. He had two airline tickets back to Los Angeles in his hand. "Joe," he said, "we shouldn't budge on our demands but if you want to forget it, I understand. I know how much you want to start playing."

"If we have to go back [to L.A.], we have to go back. I don't want to back off this one," I said. This was one of the few instances during that period when I took a hard position on anything.

Fortunately, the "trades" to Denver and Chicago moved Bill. On the Friday before camp, Bill called Larry and said he wanted to talk. They worked out the contract and I got what I wanted. I got a signing bonus of $50,000 and they threw in a cash stipend of $6,500 to cover the time the Niners worked me out with Owens.

Once I reported to training camp, things seemed to be forgotten. Not only was I relieved, but I sensed that the other coaches and players didn't get the idea that just because I'd played hardball with my first contract, I was some prima donna, a hotshot who was trying to stir things up. I was relieved, but I was scared as hell.

There were two guys who were really scared in training camp. Me and a big, friendly southerner, Dwight Clark. We were assigned to the same room and found out quickly that we were experiencing the same feelings.

We both knew that, as rookies on the 49ers, our chances of making it were questionable. Dwight never completely unpacked his suitcases. When I went out on the field and threw to him I knew how he felt when he made a good catch. He knew how I felt when I completed a pass.

Now, I'm not a backslapper, the type of person who's going to go out of my way to ingratiate myself to anyone. Dwight was the perfect counterpoint for me. He broke the ice in our relationship, trying to make things comfortable, trying to get to know me.

We started things off by again and again going over Notre Dame's win over Clemson, his alma mater. It was one of those games that kept going back and forth until the very end. It really helped to have a friend.

My first pro camp, an uncomfortable and strange environment, qualified as something that was downright frightening. I couldn't shake the feeling that people were expecting a lot of me. If I made just one mistake, it was one mistake too many. Dwight took some of the pressure off. He was comforting; we could talk openly about football and about our fears and this made the whole situation a lot easier for me.

The way Bill runs a camp is really good for a rookie's head. He tells everybody that whether you're a rookie or not, you're all 49ers until the team releases you. At that time, there were a lot of spots open for the taking. Later, as the team matured together and we won championships, it was next to impossible to win a spot on the team. That didn't stop close to a hundred rookies from coming to camp in 1985, the season following our second Super Bowl win.

Bill would hold on to a lot of these guys until the last minute. It may have done something positive for their egos to "almost" have made the 49ers. But by the time they were released it was too late for any other club to pick them up. Their careers were put on hold. That's one part of the business I find hard to stomach.

But that wasn't a problem in my rookie camp. Things were up for grabs. Rookies weren't made to feel any different. I sure felt a little different walking on the same field with the great O. J. Simpson, but there was no hazing or anything like that.

Bill would heckle rookies in a good-natured way. He would kid me about the Notre Dame–USC games, and I would joke with him about the Stanford–University of California games, which each year is "The Big Game" for both schools and is especially sacred to Bill. Near the end of my first season we were having a going-away party for O. J. Simpson, who was going to call it quits to a legendary career. The party was at a place called Harry's Hof Brau in Redwood City. We had one of the back rooms, and things were really getting lively. The booze was going down real smooth and I knew it was time for me to get out of there. Well of course I, Mr. Cautious, was overreacting: After I left nothing much happened. The veterans made all the rookies do some singing. So since I'd left early I thought I had gotten away with not singing.

On the next road trip, Bill, who is an equal-opportunity

type, wanted to make sure every rookie sang. So at a team meeting, he made me get up and sing a song that was popular in 1979, "Rapper's Delight." Believe me, I would rather throw into the teeth of the Chicago Bears' defense than sing. Well, I struggled through it. I was terrible. But that's a mild form of abuse.

Speaking of abuse, during my rookie year I was picked out for what I consider the worst job in football. No, the worst job in sports—holding for extra points and field goals. If something goes wrong, it's usually the holder's fault. Fortunately, the guy I was holding for was Ray Wersching, affectionately known to the team as "Moe"—for Mohair. Moe has so much hair on his body he looks like a little Tasmanian devil. He's not what you would call a fussy kicker. It's almost impossible to hit the spot—where the kicker wants the ball placed—on the nose. I used to hear stories where a holder would miss the spot by an inch and a kicker would walk off the field screaming about what a screw-up the holder was.

Moe was more than fair. There were times when I missed the spot or the ball spun off my hands and he'd kick and miss. He would always take the blame for it, instead of blaming it on me. That's the kind of person he is. In one game against the Rams I laid the ball flat and he kicked it anyway. Of course it was blocked, and we both took off the other way, trying to catch the man who recovered the block. I think we would have caught him sooner if we hadn't been laughing so hard.

"Why did you kick the ball?"

"Hey, Joe, I saw you holding that thing flat on the ground— I just figured I would kick it." Kickers have weird personalities, but Moe is one of a kind. Even with me holding the ball flat on the ground, he still would take the blame for it.

There was one idiot in camp my rookie year who used to tie the toe of his kicking shoe straight up in the air. He had a steel plate form-fitted for his kicking foot that ran from his shin through the ankle partway into his shoe. I thought that sucker broke my hand a few times because the steel plate hit my knuckles. Although I was new to the team, I couldn't put up with this baloney. If the dude broke my hand I was in a whole lot of trouble. "Hey, you want to hold for him?" I said to one of the coaches. "You do it. I like my hands too much." Fortunately, he couldn't kick and lasted only a few weeks.

Moe takes things seriously when it's his time to practice but he can only kick the ball so many times in practice before he gets tired. He has to do things to lighten the atmosphere. That's why I think he's so easy-going. The players know they can kid him. Once during my rookie camp Moe and I were walking through the dorm. Some of the fellows had been out at a bar and came back smashed. They jumped Moe. He began struggling, kicking and laughing. I guess he knew what they were trying to do. They tried to take his shirt off and shave the letter *M* on his back. They got him down and the shirt came off, but everyone was laughing so hard that Moe escaped. Well, one thing hadn't changed. Like the Fighting Irish, the San Francisco 49ers had their share of pranksters. Oh, another thing was similar to college: Once again I was competing for a starting slot.

The Last Competition

Steve DeBerg, who was the 49ers' starting quarterback the year before I arrived on the scene, is a heck of a competitor and as good an athlete as you're going to find anywhere. When Tampa Bay, the team he now quarterbacks, was losing week after week in 1985, I could almost feel what Steve was going through. When the Bucs decided to sign Steve Young, the high-priced quarterback from the Los Angeles Express of the USFL, I knew what he must have been thinking. He had to be dying inside.

After eight years in the NFL, I'm convinced the only thing that separates chumps from champions is the individual's competitive drive. The people who survive and then flourish—of course, having a long NFL career is an accomplishment in itself—are the ones who love to compete, maybe even live to compete.

Steve is one of these people.

I'm talking about competitive instincts that extend beyond the field. During my rookie season he had a Mattel video baseball game that we used to play. Dwight, Steve, Rickey Churchman, and I used to have tournaments all the time. When we first started playing, Steve would kill all of us. But when we got the hang of it, we would beat him. He didn't like that. When he lost he would do a lot of yelling and screaming.

I'm no different; I'll compete at anything. A couple of weeks before the '85 camp, Jen and I had some people over for a cookout. We started a game of softball and after a couple of innings my team was losing. Hey, I wasn't going around screaming at my guests, but inside I was upset. This has to be something you're born with and somehow is reinforced as you go through life. The competitive spirit was instilled in me by my mom and dad. They would ask me why the team didn't win. They'd tell me it was good to win. I was brought up disagreeing with that old saying "Winning isn't everything." I was raised to feel that winning is everything. Now, before you start criticizing that kind of thinking, you must realize one thing: The American system is built on competition, and no matter what anyone says, winners are rewarded. As long as this is the way the system is structured, then I guess it's better to operate in it successfully. Also, I've been on the bottom looking up and I don't like the feeling.

My father wasn't always telling me to win, win, win—he wasn't force-feeding me. It was more of a teaching process, and the lesson was to strive to win: to know that the only way to accomplish anything in sports is to be a winner. If a quarterback sets all kinds of individual records but plays for a losing team, the public and the media—in all their infinite wisdom—are likely to brand the guy a loser. Nobody had ever had the kind of season Dan Marino did before the Dolphins played us in the '85 Super Bowl. But he had a lousy Super Bowl. We won, and people began to doubt him. Another example is Fran Tarkenton, a great player and a successful businessman. He brought a new dimension to the quarterback position. But when people talk about his playing days they'll always wind up saying, somewhere in the conversation, that he never won a Super Bowl with the Vikings.

My competitive priorities were in proper place during my first camp, but once again my confidence was going to be put to the test. Steve went into camp as the starter. Scott Bull, who had played some in '78, was there too, so I figured they would keep him. I was there and a host of others. Bill kept bringing in other quarterbacks every week, so I figured I must not have been doing things right. At one point I even began to think that the episode with my contract may have annoyed them enough to get rid of me on the final cut.

When I'm behind I start to press, and that's what I started doing in camp. Every dropback I did during drills had to be right, correct down to the last step. Every pass had to be perfect. When you start pressing this hard it usually leads to screw-ups. But here's where the competitive edge comes in. I felt I was the best quarterback in camp. In professional football, where winning does mean everything, I figured decisions would be made on ability alone, and I had a real good shot. I relaxed a little. When I made the team, I did feel a great sense of relief.

My first season was memorable for more personal reasons. It certainly wasn't an artistic success. We went 2-14 and I only threw twenty-three passes the whole season. Of course I wanted to play more that first season, and I guess my actions and facial expressions showed it was getting to me. But I got some much-needed confidence from O. J. Simpson and Cedrick Hardman, two great veterans who really had no reason to go out of their way for me.

It's kind of an unwritten rule that most guys will leave you alone if they know you're upset. But Cedrick had been through the wars. I guess he figured that he didn't want to see someone's head messed up early in his career. One day he pulled me aside in the locker room. "Man, things aren't going to happen for you here overnight," he said. "Let me tell you this: I've been around and I can see you have what it takes. One day you are going to run this team. You'll get the chance, hang in." I just wanted to run and tell someone what Cedrick had said to me. Maybe Dwight, maybe call home, maybe go out in the street and shout it. But, in reality, I knew that this was something better kept to myself. After all those days at Notre Dame and rookie camp, someone was saying, "Joe, I believe in you." I was building an inner confidence, but getting a boost from Cedrick, a man everyone respected, was not only terrific but something that had never happened before.

It was really tough for me, and for everyone on the 49ers, to watch O.J. at the end of his career. He had always been someone I admired, through high school and college. It was really strange thinking that we were on the same team. It was like a dream. I had the same feeling early in my career when I saw Terry Bradshaw or Dan Fouts on the other side of the field. Of course with O.J. it was even better—we were teammates.

I had to laugh when I heard that Howard Cosell claimed in his last book that O.J. called him up and cried because he thought Howard was mad at him. Howard, let me dare to set you straight. Let me explain why I can't believe O.J. would have been busted up because you were mad at him. During the '79 season O.J.'s knees were in terrible shape. His instincts were there. I could see it in games. All the moves were there. They just were a split second too late. Sometimes I would think how terrible I might feel knowing my mind could play the game but my body wouldn't let me. When the backs, quarterbacks, and receivers gather to watch the film of a game it's always a time for kidding and making fun of everybody else's mistakes. No one is immune from the kidding. But one afternoon we were watching a film and O.J., in this particular game, had been caught from behind by a player who was about a half-step behind him. "Gentlemen," O.J. said, "I wasn't thinking about him. My instincts are still back in the seventies. In my own mind, I was by the guy, my mind told me that I could blow right past him. Look at the film; no one beats Father Time."

Everyone got really quiet. There wasn't a man in that room who had not been touched by the greatness of O. J. Simpson. When we heard his explanation, it hit home, and it was scary. This is something every athlete has to go through. In that film

O.J. wasn't even looking at the linebacker, he didn't try to put a move on him. Why? Because in the past he would have blown by him—his mind told him that. What is it going to be like? I wondered. What is it going to feel like when my mind tells me exactly when the pressure is coming, the exact moment to scramble out of the pocket, but my legs won't take me there?

Hell, but things weren't usually this serious, this introspective, with O.J. During that first season he provided everyone with a lot of laughs. We knew he was retiring, and as the season wound down he wasn't playing that much because he was so banged up he could hardly run. In practice, he would sometimes go in motion the wrong way. Let's face it, he didn't really need to pick up all the new things Bill would install from week to week. Also, we were losing so much, that practice—which basically is boring even if you're winning—was real drudgery. O.J. and Cedrick would try their best to liven things up. O.J. would be looking all serious going through the plays and Cedrick would begin getting on him. "Hey, O.J., get in there and show us all how to go in motion the wrong way, please?" Cedrick would say. "Come on, show us how to do it right."

When it came to livening up a losers' locker room, there was nobody better than O.J. We had a defensive lineman with a severe case of halitosis—bad breath in layman's terms. This was sometime after the Scope mouthwash advertising campaign depicted a phantom who would leave a bottle of Scope with someone who had bad breath.

One afternoon O.J. came into the locker room riding on the back of big Al Cowlings. Both of them had towels covering their noses and mouths. They deposited a monster-size bottle of Scope in the bad-breath guy's locker. The two phantoms then rode off to take a shower.

When the defensive lineman came back to his locker he freaked. He was ready to kill whoever had deposited that bottle and was accusing everybody. Things got nasty and a fight almost broke out. While all the screaming and shouting was going on, O.J. and Al dressed, huge grins on their faces. How could it have been them? the lineman must have thought. They were in the shower all the time.

O.J. had the ability to make people relax. He kidded everyone and they seemed to enjoy it. He is the kind of guy who also could be kidded. In fact, I think he got a lot of his material from pranks and jokes that had been played on him.

Knowing all this, I was still shocked when he came over and talked to me. I shouldn't have been; O.J. treated everyone on the team the same. That was one of the great things about him. I remember the first time I met him. I was walking by and he asked me to sit down. Juice just started talking. "God, what is he doing talking to me?" I thought. "Why would he want to?" That was just O.J.'s way, and believe me, I really appreciated him.

There were other things that I began to appreciate. Of course I wanted to play my rookie season, but I came to realize that I would have been torn apart if I had played. No matter how much inner confidence I had, we were being beaten badly. Not only might I have taken a mental beating, but I probably would have taken a physical one as well.

Bill elected to hold me out. When he did put me in a game during my first two years, it would be when we were in the other team's territory and on our way to score. Once, in my second year, we were playing the Cowboys, and they were beating the crap out of us, something like 50–7. Bill kept looking back at the bench for people to put in the game. Occasionally, he looked at me and, I must admit, I was scared. I didn't want to go in, so every time he looked around, I turned my back on him. But he didn't want to put me in either. He was breaking me in slowly. Bill didn't want to throw me to the lions right away because he had seen the careers of some pretty good players destroyed that way. There's nothing as frightening as playing against a defense who know you must pass to win. You walk up to the line of scrimmage, look at the defense, and see these big guys loading up. You might as well be the matador's red cape because the defensive linemen are definitely bulls, but no one is yelling *"¡ole!"* The linemen are down in sprinters' stances, digging in. They're on a one-way mission, a runaway stampede for my bones. Let's face it: It's a race to see who will be the first guy to kick my butt.

It's no fun sitting back there in a vulnerable position. I've got to have faith in the five or six guys who protect me. In my first two years, our offensive line—which will no doubt go down as one of the greatest offensive lines of the 1980s—was just coming together, just learning about each other's moves. More often than not the quarterback was a sitting duck. So Bill would definitely pick his spots for me. Coming into my rookie year, I wasn't throwing the ball real well; I was throwing OK—not good enough to impress anyone—but OK.

Bill was holding me out because he was looking toward the future. A rookie who is thrown into the heat of NFL competition can come out both mentally and physically scarred. I think that's what happened to Jack Thompson, a gutsy quarterback who was respected and loved by everyone in football. He played in Tampa Bay and Cincinnati. He was so damn respected by his peers but, of course, was picked on by the media. Hell, they didn't know what Jackie was going through. He was getting his ass kicked every Sunday while these dudes pontificated for free in the comfort of the press box.

I was lucky. Bill was grooming me to become the 49ers' quarterback of the future—I hoped! During my second training camp I was throwing better and developing some real confidence. It was the start of believing in myself as a pro. Steve DeBerg was getting the worst end of the deal. I'm sure he was having a tough time living with the fact that although he was playing, I was waiting in the wings to take his job.

I felt bad for Steve; he was my friend. Bill might have been handpicking situations for me to build my confidence but what was that doing to DeBerg? Inside he must have been going nuts, but he never said anything. He never complained. He had to believe he was better than me but even if he didn't, he was too much of a competitor to ever admit it.

The way they were treating Steve would have driven me

crazy. He'd be putting together a good drive and Bill would pull him out of the game and put me in. During my rookie year, in a game against the New York Jets, Steve took us to the 5-yard line and Bill pulled him so I could score the touchdown. That season, football for me was played inside the opponent's 50-yard line.

I was learning a new system, and when you get right down to it, that's the hardest transition a college quarterback has to make as a professional. If there was ever a mental turning point in my career, it was during my first two seasons. Although I wasn't playing regularly, I was taking a lot of time to learn the 49ers' system. If I hadn't put in that time I wouldn't have developed into a quality NFL quarterback.

Besides learning our system I was also trying to understand the new defenses that were out there. The 49ers' numbering system of plays was totally different from Notre Dame's, where the "numbers" of plays were pass patterns. With the 49ers, the numbers are blocking assignments except when they are used as audibles.

For example, the numbers in the 49ers' system tell you which back is going to stay in and block and which one isn't. The words the quarterback says after that number tell you which pass route is going to be run. Learning all this is hard and time-consuming. The only way to do it is to memorize it and try to get used to which back is staying in and which one is releasing to run a pass pattern. This is what I tried to get down first; learning the patterns came after that.

The combination of learning all Bill's plays and the pressure of being a rookie, well, it was tough. If you show the coaches you don't know the plays, they're not going to let you into a game. I concentrated on learning the receivers' moves and idiosyncrasies. Figuring out when each one starts to break down and break out takes time. It was a crash course in sharpening my instincts. Each receiver on the 49ers is reading the defense. I've learned to guess and anticipate where they are going so I can throw to the open area.

Becoming a good passer really depends on getting used to

receivers. Each man does something different before he makes his break. I was learning routes—where receivers can hook, cross, or come back to the ball. When they are going into the inside, I throw the ball harder. When a receiver is going inside over the middle, it's not a good time to take anything off the ball. They're going into a dangerous territory. It's a place where the head can be separated from the body. I always try to make it easy for the receiver but, unfortunately, I don't always have time to do that. In the end, I realized that to be a good pro passer you must be some sort of a psychic.

You have to be able to tell what's on a receiver's mind by the way he's running a route. If you can anticipate his break, you're going to be a step ahead of the defense.

With that great body of knowledge behind me, I prepared to start my first game, our third exhibition game of the season, against the Denver Broncos at Candlestick. We lost 21–0. I went twelve for twenty with two interceptions.

But the game I'll never forget was the following exhibition game against the Seattle Seahawks. The Kingdome, home of the Seahawks, is an enormous place. When I walked into the dome I began getting nervous. No, nervous doesn't accurately describe my feelings. I was scared to death.

I was lucky that I didn't eat much before the game because I would have tossed my cookies on the sideline. The place swallowed me up. The fans were noisy and nasty. They certainly didn't care that this was my second pro start. In fact, they did their best to make it my last. I hung in during the first half. Although we were losing 34–0, I didn't throw any interceptions. But in the second half I began pressing. Somehow I had to get us back in the game. That was a big mistake. On our first series we had the ball first and 10 on our 32-yard line. I dropped back to pass and forced one right into the hands of Seattle's defensive back Autry Beaman. Autry wasn't satisfied with just running the ball back for a score; he had other things in mind: pain and humiliation. I was the only person between Autry and the goal line. Did he try to fake his way around me? Did he turn on the speed to outrun me? No, I might as well not have been out there. Autry ran me over on his way to a touchdown.

This wasn't the end of the "Bury Joe Show." On the next series I was faced with a third and 11 from our 17-yard line. I forced another pass right into the hands of another DB, Dave Brown. He ran the ball back 32 yards for a touchdown. At least he was courteous and didn't run me over. We lost the game 48–0.

So you still want to be an NFL quarterback?

7

The Dream That Didn't Die:
A Championship

When I walk to the line of scrimmage and stick my hands under our center Fred Quillan, things happen automatically. If I ever stopped to think about what happens, what really makes things tick, after the ball hits my hands, it might screw up the whole process. Why? Because things happen so fast I would be amazed at my reaction time.

When you think about that, it's really no different from anyone else who pursues a profession seriously. I guess if a surgeon has performed open-heart surgery a few hundred times, he's going to do certain intricate things instinctively; there's no great mystery to that.

What the 49ers did in 1981 is still something that I like to sit back and reflect on. It was mind-boggling. We were stone-cold losers my first two years, including our 6-10 record in 1980. How did we win? Why did we turn it around? When you compare our rebuilding process with that of other teams you realize ours was legitimate. The newspapers in some cities report that their teams are rebuilding, but it's not genuine. For instance, the New York media thought the Jets' rebuilding process the same year was for real. It wasn't. The players knew it.

But our development was. Don't let anyone pull the wool over your eyes. The key to winning in the NFL is having a dominant offensive line. Ours was coming together in 1980, but it clicked in 1981. They had been working together for a few years and now they were ready. It's true that the game is won up front, and our line—John Ayers, Randy Cross, Keith Fahnhorst (also known as Farnie), Fred Quillan, and Dan Audick—came of age in 1981.

Another key piece to our success was our defensive backfield: Ronnie Lott, Dwight Hicks, Carlton Williamson, and Eric Wright. Maybe they didn't reach their full potential in '81, but they were so aggressive they gained a whole lot of respect and were feared by most of the receivers who went up against them.

One other key was an intangible. No one tried to take credit for what was happening. This is really important if a team is going to win.

Bill's decision to trade Steve DeBerg helped me psychologically. Prior to '81 I wondered when I was going to get my chance to start. I also felt guilty that Steve was being used until Bill felt I was ready. At the start of '81, Bill told me I was going to be the number-one quarterback, but I had my doubts. In the past he had hinted I would start, but with Steve around I figured it would be another season of us going back and forth. When Bill traded Steve, I knew the job was mine.

Before the season, I figured one of us was going to go. Our personalities were so similar that keeping us both around would have led to friction. We both had to play to be happy. So, Steve's departure was a relief, but at the same time I was sad. You don't make that many close friends with people on the team, and Steve was still a close friend.

I never worried about being traded those first couple of years. I guess it was the way Bill used me. It made me realize that I would eventually get the job. I had to. After I signed with the 49ers I didn't make any alternative plans. One way or another, my life was going to be football. My confidence soared when Steve was traded.

The 1981 season started off like the two previous ones. We

lost our first two games. But there was a difference in our attitude during those losses. Previously, we would go into games hoping we would just make it through and perform respectably. We didn't want to make fools out of ourselves. And in 1980 it was just a matter of time before the dam would burst and the 49ers would be blown out.

The big difference in '81 was that we developed confidence. We went into games knowing we could win. If our opponents weren't aggressive, or didn't take us seriously, we knew we would beat them. It's hard to explain why a team can begin feeling this way in the space of a year. Much of it comes from what you see in your teammates. Everyone feeds off each other's strengths.

Our offensive line was an example. I would drop back to pass and see our guard John Ayers battling a defensive lineman. All of a sudden a linebacker or safety would be coming on a blitz. John's instincts and experience had come together to such a point where he could still be blocking and be able to turn his body to pick up the blitz and knock the defender off stride at the same time. This would give me time to throw the ball. In '81 our entire offensive line was playing together, and they were a confident unit. It was beautiful.

They were like a good basketball team. Blocking is a lot like making those switches when you're playing a man-to-man defense. If you don't have the confidence that every opponent will be covered, your team's in trouble. It's the same with the offensive line. The guys have to know when to let a defender come right through. They have to be confident enough in their linemates to know a defender will be picked up before he gets to the quarterback.

When I realized our line had come together, I knew we were set for a run at the Super Bowl. A golfer or tennis player can win it by himself. A quarterback, despite what a lot of people think, can't. Now all the parts seemed to be working. The offensive line and our defense were confident in what they could do. Our running game wasn't going to tear anybody up but it was adequate.

And of course there was D.C., Dwight Clark. He came into his own that season. He had an outstanding year, but his success led to some misconceptions about my on-the-field relationship with him. The fans and the press believed I was looking for him because of our friendship. They thought we had this special chemistry because we were friends. This was not true. Friendship had nothing to do with Dwight getting the ball as much as he did. Sure, I had a lot of confidence in him. But if you look at the plays Bill was calling, it's clear that I wasn't the only one who had confidence in D.C. If we had a third down and 4 yards to go or third and 8, Dwight would come up with 10. He would always get you that first down. We didn't have any secret communication between us. There were no mystical football antennae. In fact, there wasn't a whole lot of communication needed. His ability was the key. There's not much to do when a receiver is standing out there wide open. Just get the damn ball to him.

My confidence in what he could do on the field grew that season. But DeBerg would have done the same thing. When the chips were down Dwight was going to be in there fighting. Personalities and friends mean nothing when you get on the field. You could despise a receiver, but if he's open you're going to go to him. You get him the ball any way you can. That's part of being a professional.

The press didn't understand this. They believed Montana-to-Clark was a pass combination born purely out of friendship. That's a fairy tale. I look for the open man and Dwight was the guy. But I guess if I was throwing the ball to Freddie Solomon all the time that year, the press would have come up with some reason for that too.

Another myth that should have been put in cold storage that season was my ability to throw the long pass. People have always suspected that I have a weak arm. But if they look back to '81, they will see we were throwing the ball long with success. We had to move the ball down the field with longer passes because our running game wasn't consistent.

Things just fell into place for us in '81. When one thing didn't work, another would. When our offense faltered, our defense picked things up. I realize now that we didn't even come close to our potential as a football team that season. At the time I honestly didn't realize what was happening to me or the 49ers. We kept winning and I was kind of afraid to look ahead at the schedule. Would the bubble burst? When I saw the teams we had to play, I didn't think we could keep it up.

If I lacked confidence in winning it all, our defensive backs—especially Ronnie Lott—didn't. He played his college ball at USC, a school that breeds hard-hitting defensive backs. Ronnie has to be the hardest hitter the Trojans ever produced. You would be hard pressed to find four guys in the league who hit harder than our DBs!—even those big bad Chicago Bears.

It's amazing that, with the exception of Dwight Hicks, who we picked up in '79, our entire defensive backfield was plucked from the '81 draft. No one is going to try to intimidate or mess with any of these fellows, especially Ronnie. Not only are they hard hitters but they are a studious bunch. Our defensive coach, George Seifert, expects them to watch more films and sit in class more than any other group on the team. It's like they're back in college. Despite this classroom atmosphere off the field, they definitely go from Jekyll to Hyde on game day. They became known as "Dwight Hicks and the Hot Licks." During that first Super Bowl season, Carlton Williamson knocked two Pittsburgh Steeler receivers—John Stallworth and Cal Sweeney—out of a game with vicious hits. During that game, they forced six turnovers that keyed a 17–14 win for us. But Ronnie is the hub of the secondary. He's not Mr. Finesse, he is the hit man. He plays like a smart Fred "The Hammer" Williamson, a hard hitter who played for the Kansas City Chiefs in the early years of the American Football League.

Before each game we gather to say the Lord's Prayer. Most players get anxious to hit the field, especially when we're playing on the road. When Ronnie's ready he wants to go—no holdups, no waiting, for Mr. Lott. He can get very excited on game day and at times display quite a temper. In '81 we were on the road playing Atlanta. Our locker room was split into two rooms.

Well, the coaches were trying to get us into one room to say the prayer without much success. Ronnie didn't appreciate the delay and took things into his own hands. "Goddamn it, everybody get up here, get in this goddamn room so we can say the goddamn Lord's Prayer and get out on the goddamn field," he screamed. What do you think happened? Everyone moved. Once he got on the field he was still mad. He was tossed out of the game for punching Atlanta receiver Alfred Jackson.

One of my favorite characters is Freddie Solomon, or as we call him, Casper the Friendly Ghost. When Freddie was traded to the 49ers from the Miami Dolphins in '78 we found out that his Miami teammates called him Casper because his shadow looked like a ghost. Freddie is a sensitive guy, whose emotions can go up and down pretty fast. I've never thrown to a receiver with the speed he has. He's not known around the league as a real burner but I would bet a few bucks on him in a foot race with some people who are considered among the quickest receivers in the NFL. Freddie announced his retirement in 1985, and I'm going to miss him. As far as I'm concerned, he could still add to our offense. I suspect he will end up playing with another team. I think he wants to go back to Tampa and end his career in his hometown.

I got the feeling that Bill never fully appreciated Freddie. Freddie would get lazy every now and then and run a bad route at the wrong time. Sometimes he wouldn't practice when Bill thought he should. But when the chips were down Freddie Solomon played his butt off. He was terribly underrated.

Freddie had always wanted to be a quarterback. At the University of Tampa he was an exciting QB. He rushed for thirty-nine TDs and passed for eleven. He was voted the offensive player of the game in the East-West Shrine game in his senior year and was drafted in the second round by the Dolphins in 1975.

Although he was drafted fairly high, there was no way he was going to play quarterback for the Dolphins. He had a lot of speed, and Don Shula, Miami's head coach, had it in his mind that Freddie had to be converted into a wide receiver. Don leveled with Freddie. He told him he had no chance of playing quarterback in the NFL. Freddie told me that he'd desperately wanted to play quarterback but came to the realization that it wasn't going to happen. It was something he had to live with throughout his career. He put his pride in his back pocket.

Freddie was surprised when Miami traded him to San Francisco in '78. It was as if they didn't want him anymore. The whole thing surprised him. He came to the 49ers with severe knee problems. He told me that his knees hurt him so bad that he sometimes wanted to take himself out of the game. He was too proud to give up.

I couldn't understand why Freddie had hand problems. His hobby is carving intricate wood sculptures. One of his most impressive is called *Moses and the Ten Commandments.* Bill worked with Freddie, who had a habit of improvising his routes. He then began to realize that if he made it to the spot where the play was called, I could get the ball to him quite easily.

And Bill soon realized that he was dealing with a group of men who had unique personalities. He tolerated everyone's quirks because we meshed. We had no one who craved the spotlight. When we started to win we took it in stride. To keep winning we needed everyone pulling together, doing their jobs. Everyone had to concentrate on performing, not bullshitting. No one player could carry the team. As the season progressed, our youth and aggressiveness paid off. None of us had ever been through anything like this before.

We didn't think about it too much. The key was taking one game at a time. Early in the season the 49ers ambushed people because we were taken lightly. Suddenly, as we gained momentum, we were taken seriously. By this time it was too late for the rest of the league. We had taken everyone by surprise. Whatever insecurities we had had disappeared. We were for real.

My teammates were making me feel secure and I returned the favor. This was what I had been pointing to since my days with the Monongahela Little Wildcats, my peewee team, and my practice sessions with Dad. I knew our offensive line was going to give me time to throw the ball. They also knew if a block was missed I had the ability to run out of trouble. It was funny. We had had the same pieces that could make a winner in '80. The difference was the confidence wasn't there. Nothing would come together for us.

I knew something big was happening when we went on the road and kept on winning. The game that stands out in my mind was our 17–14 win over Pittsburgh. When I entered the NFL and found myself on the same field with Dan Fouts or Terry Bradshaw, I was living a dream. I would pinch myself. These gentlemen were my heroes. As a kid I really didn't have any idols. I liked Joe Namath and I was a big Kansas City Chiefs and Len Dawson fan. I also was a Steelers fan but there was no time for me to really follow pro football—I was too busy playing.

Although our family didn't live far from Three Rivers Stadium, home of the Steelers, I never went to a Pittsburgh game. The first time I saw the Steelers live was when the 49ers played them. This was so special to me. Not only was I going home as the starting quarterback of a darn good team, but if the 49ers could win I would conquer a mental obstacle and give myself a super shot of confidence. To say I was in awe of the Pittsburgh Steelers was, and still is, an understatement. After all, I knew about the Pittsburgh legend and how much the team meant to the people of western Pennsylvania. When I fantasize about playing for another team it's always the Steelers. They still had a lot of the players from their 1980 Super Bowl team. As far as I was concerned, if we could go into Pittsburgh and beat them, we were good enough to win it all. They were our litmus test. I had a poor day and so did the 49ers, but we played well enough to win.

As we moved late into the season, something weird was developing. We were winning but everyone was on edge. A lot of it had to do with the San Francisco media. The sportswriters were so conditioned to covering losers that they were behind us in a funny kind of way. Their stories indicated they were just waiting for the bottom to fall out. They were definitely hedging their bets. If we took a fall, the San Francisco media wanted to be the first to say, "We told you so."

They were wrong. We were going to make the playoffs. As the playoffs approached, things were getting scary, a little on the surreal side. The national media was beginning to focus on the 49ers as a team and on me personally. Losers had suddenly become winners. People from all over the country were following us. I was in my first season as a starter but all of a sudden I was getting tremendous recognition. Nothing at Notre Dame ever compared to this. The spotlight was as bright as a Hawaiian sunset, but the attention didn't affect the 49ers.

We were taking everything in stride. We had no preconceived notions of what a trip through the playoffs would be like. All we knew was that we had something to prove. Deep down inside, each and every one of us knew we had a great chance to go to the Super Bowl. We finished the regular season with a 13-3 record. The previous year we had been 6-10. Since the NFL underwent its restructuring in 1970, no team had shown that kind of improvement.

First we had to deal with the New York Giants, a team we had beaten 17–10 earlier in the season. Bill was playing all the angles. He knew that the New York team was going to come into a playoff game super pumped. "We beat them," he said. "but it gives us absolutely no psychological advantage. When you get to the playoffs, you start over. It's another season. Throw out scores and stats."

This blunted the hostile feelings the Giants had for us. They were getting it from two sides. There were a couple of reasons for this. The New York fanatics and media are perennially starved for a winning team. They get behind the Giants and go berserk. Sometimes I wonder if it's the fans' own way of blowing off steam, taking out their aggressions from a tough day of work at a football game in Giants Stadium. If the Giants make the playoffs, they go crazy. This gives a team a false sense of security. Bill pounced on this theory and began making public statements. It had rained heavily in San Francisco the week before the game, forcing us to practice indoors. Bill said in an interview that this could hamper us. We knew damn well we were ready to go. We could have been practicing on Pluto and it wouldn't have made a difference.

Then there was the matter of Fred Dean. Fred would turn down a sneaker endorsement in order to letter the tape covering his shoes with his nickname, "The Warrior." He was the ultimate sack machine, dedicated to twisting necks, chewing them up, and spitting them out. In another interview, Bill said that the Giants held Fred on purpose during that first game, pulled Fred down by the face mask and tackled him. The player Bill was talking about was my fellow Notre Dame alumnus Jeff Weston. When we beat them during the regular season, Weston was holding Fred on every play, at least according to Bill.

He also played the rain angle for all it was worth. A couple of times he was asked about what Candlestick's turf might look like when the tarp was pulled off after the monsoon season hit. "There's no telling what we'll find when we raise the tarpaulin," he said. "A lot of fishing worms, I guess."

I stayed away from talking although I had no love for the Giants. There were two reasons I felt we would win the game. John Ayers would be blocking Lawrence Taylor on all pass plays. There was no doubt that John could do what no one else could in the NFL—keep L.T. off the quarterback. On running plays, Bill had another plan to contain Taylor. Charle Young, our tight end, would anticipate Taylor's pursuit and just wait for him, sit back and drill him. If this worked, Taylor wouldn't be a factor in the game.

Wouldn't you know it, when we walked on the field for the game it was raining. This was a good omen. I even rubbed my hand in the slimy Candlestick turf to check for worms. We came out flying. I knew we had to get off fast and we did. We went 85 yards in thirteen plays. But things weren't all that smooth on the drive. I and my "weak" arm connected with Ricky Patton for a 64-yard touchdown, but the play was called back when Freddie was called for clipping their defensive back, Mark Haynes. It's funny, things always have a way of evening out. What goes around comes around. On the same drive we had a fourth and 23, which forced us to punt. Fortunately, Haynes was caught holding, and we kept the ball. We finally ended the drive with an 8-yard touchdown pass to Charle Young.

We were up 7–0 early, but I knew the Giants were in a nasty mood. They weren't going to lie down and die. They moved 72 yards in two plays. Their quarterback, Scott Brunner, hit Earnest Gray with a 72-yard pass to tie the game. There was still 12:15 left in the first quarter. I figured the team that scored last would win.

We came back in the second quarter, going 45 yards in eight plays that ended when Moe hit a 22-yard field goal.

Then it was Ronnie Lott time. After the Giants got the ball, Ronnie intercepted a Brunner pass that Dwight Hicks tipped—it would be the first of two Lott interceptions—setting us up for a 58-yard pass to Freddie and a 17–7 lead. I still didn't feel comfortable. Everyone was loose and anything could happen. Things started to change after that score. We took the momentum from the Giants. Leon Bright fumbled Moe's kickoff and Keena Turner recovered on the Giants' 42-yard line. It took us three plays to score on Ricky Patton's 25-yard run. Suddenly we had a 24–7 lead. We had scored 17 points in four minutes and thirty-three seconds.

I'm sure our fans believed the butt kicking was under way. But I had a queasy feeling in my stomach. Something told me the Giants would come back. They didn't disappoint me.

Joey Danelo, their placekicker, hit a 48-yard field goal late in the second quarter, cutting our lead to 24–10. During halftime I wondered if they could actually steal the momentum from us. They did. Bill Currier intercepted my pass and it only took one play, a 59-yard pass from Scott to Johnny Perkins, to make it a 24–17 game. Suddenly it was gut-check time.

For the uninitiated, "gut check" is when an athlete is faced with a crucial situation: a win-or-lose proposition. Simply stated, does the athlete have the guts and nerve to handle the crisis? The next time the Giants got the ball they moved to our 11-yard line. Rob Carpenter ran it to our 2. Suddenly the Giants were in complete charge. Brunner dropped back to pass and threw a sound-barrier pass, I mean, low, hard, and screaming, to Earnest Gray. He caught the ball about a foot short of the goal line but he didn't anticipate Eric Wright stripping the ball out of his hands, turning a touchdown into an incomplete pass. Danelo felt the pressure and missed the 21-yard chippie.

In the fourth quarter Freddie lifted our spirits with a 24-yard punt return. I completed a first-down pass but it went nowhere. We took a 4-yard loss. Things got worse. On the next play we were penalized 15 yards for holding.

But then our break came. Sometimes you just get lucky. Sometimes the mental factor takes over. I hit on a 6-yard pass but we were faced with a third and 18 at the Giants' 41-yard line. As the players were returning to the huddle, Gary Jeter, the Giants defensive end, and Dan Audick, our offensive tackle, got into a shoving contest. Jeter was caught throwing the last punch and was penalized 15 yards for unnecessary roughness. This gave us an automatic first down, keeping the drive alive.

It took us four plays to score. Billy Ring, our all-purpose spiritual leader, who will do anything for the team, scored from 3 yards out, giving us a 31–17 lead. The Jeter penalty completely changed the face of the game. The game went from intense matchup to garbage time. Ronnie intercepted a Brunner pass and ran 20 yards for a touchdown, making the score 38–17, with 11:49 left in the game.

The Giants didn't quit. They showed class. Brunner hit Perkins for a 17-yard score, but it was too late. We killed the clock. Suddenly we were on our way to the NFC Championship game.

Bring on "America's Team," the Dallas Cowboys.

We had a week to prepare for the Cowboys' defense which, at that time, was known as "Doomsday II." The Cowboys had slipped a little. Earlier in the season we had beaten them pretty badly, 45–14, but they didn't just have revenge on their minds. They were also high because they'd whipped Tampa Bay 38–0 in the NFC semifinal. They had the sentimentality factor going for them. This could be their great linebacker, D. D. Lewis's final game as a Cowboy. D.D. planned to retire following the season. He would be breaking the record for most playoff appearances—twenty-six—which he shared with his former roommate Larry Cole. D.D. knew we'd caught the Cowboys by surprise when we leveled them earlier in the season. They had been super confident and we had caught them thinking, not reacting. They were standing back on their heels, trying to figure out if they were in the right defensive formation. They were thinking too much.

Going into the playoff, we were pretty banged up. Keena Turner had a mild case of the chicken pox and was isolated from the team for two days. Marcus Welby, where were you when we needed you? Keith Fahnhorst was recovering from a mild case of the flu but was gaining his strength back. We needed Farnie. He would be taking on Ed "Too Tall" Jones, the Cowboys' left end and the guy most likely to be in my face all day. Dallas also had their problems. John Dutton, their left defensive tackle, was not likely to play. He had broken a blood vessel in his left thigh and was questionable. The injury list didn't stop. Our running back Ricky Patton sprained his ankle and wasn't going to play. We would miss Ricky, but that season we were a passing team, and the running backs weren't a key to our game plan.

Bill believed it would be a high-scoring game. He told me we needed to score at least four touchdowns to win. I agreed. In my mind the key to the game was stopping their pass rush. Although their Doomsday defense were on their last legs, they were proud. One gentleman who I knew was looking forward to the game was Harvey Martin. "Beautiful" Harvey hadn't played against us in the regular season, and I knew he was itching to get a shot at me. People were writing him off, saying he didn't have it anymore. I knew better. The Beautiful One would be coming at me from "Planet Violence." Fortunately, he would be going up against Dan Audick, who had had a good game against Gary Jeter in the Giants game. This had to boost Danny's confidence.

I wasn't going to single out any defender. Hell, I knew they all wanted to kick my tail. If I could get rid of the ball quickly, read their defense in a hurry, and execute to the max, we would win.

During the week of the game, Tom Callahan, *Time* magazine's sportswriter, was working on a story about me. Tom told me that if we beat Dallas my picture would be on the cover of *Time* the week before the Super Bowl. If we didn't win, his story would be spiked. If a nonsports magazine wanted to put me on the cover, the 49ers' story must be capturing someone's attention. Well, we still had to penetrate Doomsday, and that was no lock by any stretch of the imagination.

The bad blood was flowing. Too Tall Jones was quoted as saying he had no respect for the 49ers. Even though we had beaten them badly, he said he had no respect for us. Ed intimated that our entire season had been a fluke.

There was a euphoric atmosphere at Candlestick Park before the Dallas game. The fans had waited a long time, a lot longer than any of the players, for a shot at the title. The noise level was high, and came in waves. We were relaxed. I was as comfortable as I could be under the circumstances.

The only time I ever feel pressure is during the pregame at the hotel, because there I can feel everyone else's tension. On the road that feeling was usually relieved for me by the sight of our great linebacker Jack "Hacksaw" Reynolds. Hacksaw would come to breakfast fully dressed in his uniform. He would eat quickly and split for the stadium. Seeing a guy eating scrambled eggs in shoulder pads tickled me. On the field things never bother me. If I am having a personal problem or there is a ruckus being raised in the stadium, I'm able to put it out of my mind. I have things so fine-tuned that I believe Candlestick could be engulfed in flames and it wouldn't matter. As long as everyone was still playing, I wouldn't even notice the smoke.

Our mental preparation is intensified by Bill's scripting the first twenty-five plays. In '81, no one paid much attention to our script. The system worked well for me because I knew just what I had to do when we had the ball.

Against Dallas, things got off to a fast start. We took the lead and I surprised myself. I usually don't like to say anything to the defense. But on this occasion I was damned mad about Too Tall's remark that he didn't respect us.

If I read something with quotation marks around it, more often than not I believe it. Like any other player, I want to be respected by my peers. Anyway, during that opening drive I did a waggle. That's when we fake a sweep one way and don't block the defensive end who is on the side of the field I'm running toward. I'm out there naked and have to fake around the defender. In this case it was Godzilla, my buddy Too Tall.

We wanted to draw Too Tall inside of me with a fake so I could get around him and throw the ball. The Cowboys called an inside blitz. Too Tall was on the outside looping.

This was really bad. He didn't buy the fake. There I was out there, naked as baby Alexandra, face to face with an angry giant. In a couple of seconds he was going to transform me into a bowl of Cream of Wheat. In a situation like this, my instincts take complete control. Too Tall charged and I took a hard step up to the outside. My only salvation was to make him think I was going to attempt to run around him. Fortunately for me and my rib cage, he went for the fake. This gave me time to duck underneath him and complete a 30-yard pass to Dwight.

I turned around and saw Too Tall getting up off the ground. "Respect that, big man!" I screamed.

The words were heartfelt. Believe me, I had to be pretty mad to utter those words. It was stupid and out of character for me to say that, or anything, to the opponents on the field. Too Tall was going to have a number of chances to decapitate me. I just felt I needed to gain his respect. It wouldn't hurt to give him something to think about.

AUDIBLES: MY LIFE IN FOOTBALL

Randy Cross, our right guard, wasn't happy with my mouth-ing off. "Joe, just shut the hell up and play," he said. I should have known better. Randy was one of the guys who would feel Too Tall's wrath. It didn't make Randy's job any easier, dealing with an irate Ed Jones. The Cowboys came right back to score when Danny White led a 44-yard, nine-play drive. The key play was White hitting Butch Johnson for 20 yards, setting up a 44-yard Rafael Septien field goal and a 7–3 score. The Cowboys were clicking. Mike Hegman recovered a Billy Ring fumble at our 29. It took Danny only two plays to hit Tony Hill with a 20-yard pass, giving the Cowboys a 10–7 lead.

We remained calm; there was a lot of time left in the game. I even tried a long fade for a quick score but it was intercepted by Everson Walls. Our defense held and I got another shot. This time I hit Dwight with a 26-yard pass to put us ahead 14–10. We went 47 yards in seven plays. The big play that set us up was a 12-yard pass to Freddie.

Dallas came back to score late in the second quarter. Things looked like they were going to break right for us when Ronnie Lott intercepted a Danny White pass. But the interception was wiped out when Ronnie was called for a 35-yard pass interfer-ence. Tony Dorsett then capitalized on the interference call, quickly scoring from 5 yards out and putting them up 17–14.

And that's how the first half ended. We felt we were lucky to be down by only 3 points.

Bill was calm in the locker room. There were no speeches; we just went over our assignments for the second half. The 49ers had come this far. There was no reason to change our halftime routine.

The third quarter was all defense. No one could score until one of White's passes was intercepted by Bobby Leopold. The interception set up Johnny Davis's 2-yard touchdown run, which gave us a 21–17 lead going into the fourth quarter. Now it was nervous time. One quarter left and the season was on the line. My mind was running the 100-yard dash the way bullet Bobby Hayes, the great Cowboy, did in his prime.

Dear God, please give me the ball. The game was in our

hands to win. Somehow we controlled our excitement. We played on an even keel and didn't panic. We were a reflection of Bill, never getting too high or too low. The legend, the Dallas Cowboys, began to push. There was no doubt they had reached a point that would set the tone for their franchise for the next decade. A loss would leave a deep scar. They put their foot on the pedal and jammed it through the floorboard.

Early in the fourth quarter, the Cowboys went on a quick— exactly fifty-two-second—drive ending on a 22-yard Septien field goal. The play setting up the kick was a 28-yard pass-interference call on Ronnie. Now we had a 21–20 lead.

Then we made a critical mistake and, of course, Everson Walls was there to capitalize. We fumbled the ball at midfield. The Cowboys didn't waste any time going the 50 yards in. The two big plays in the drive were an 11-yard run by Tony Dorsett and Danny's 11-yard pass to Ron Springs. This put the ball at our 21-yard line and Danny hit his great tight end Doug Cosbie for a touchdown. The Cowboys had a 27–21 lead with 4:19 left in our season.

Now it was super gut-check time. I felt numb. I heard no noise. I didn't know where I was or who we were playing. All I saw was 89 yards between us and the end zone. I didn't walk into the huddle and do any screaming. In my mind I knew we could take care of business. When our offense walked on the field we, at that moment, became a mature football team.

I saw something that surprised me. The Cowboys had a defense on the field designed to stop the pass. Six defensive backs and only one linebacker. I knew this was a mistake on their part. I also knew that Bill would pick it up. He was going to run the heck out of Lenvil Elliot. Lenvil was going to shove the ball down Doomsday's throat.

Lenvil ran four of our first eight plays, gaining 24 yards. I saw confusion on the faces of the Dallas defense. Lenvil was chewing up chunks of yardage and Dallas wasn't making any adjustments.

Then came the big play. We ran a double reverse to Freddie. He took off, moving the ball from the Cowboys' 49 to their 39. I sensed that Freddie wanted the ball again and I went right back to him for a 12-yard gain. We had crossed up the Cowboys again, going away from the run to the pass. Suddenly we were on the 6-yard line.

On second down, I missed Freddie for the go-ahead touchdown.

Now there were fifty-eight seconds left in the game. Again, I flashed back. The word *choke* kept passing through my mind. Despite this perfectly executed drive, I knew if we lost we would be just another bunch of choke artists, Apple Annies, guys who came so far only to fold during gut-check time.

The Cowboys called time-out to set their defense. When I came over to the sideline to talk with Bill he was doing his usual thing—talking into his headset to our coaches in the press box. When Bill gets off the horn in a crucial situation, he usually stresses one point. He wanted the pass to Freddie again. The situation kind of reminded me of Devine in the Cotton Bowl with Kris Haines.

"Joe, be very cautious," Walsh warned. "It's only third down. If we miss on this one we still have another shot at putting it in."

"If it's not there," I said, "I'll put it up so no one will catch the ball. Bill, don't worry, I'll be careful."

I dropped back and was pressured by three Cowboys. I don't even remember who they were. My concentration level had never been so high. It's funny how the mind takes over.

Running to my right to chill the heat, I saw Dwight cutting across the end zone. One pump fake. Hey, it was just like basketball with Dad. A fake would usually get him up in the air when we went one-on-one in the playground. It worked this time too. The fake got the guys rushing me off the floor, buying me a tiny bit more time to throw.

I was off balance and falling back. There was only one kind of pass to throw: Put the sucker up high and hard. Ideally this would not only get the ball over the human clothesline that formed around me, but it would likely guarantee that if D.C. didn't catch the ball no one else would.

When Dwight caught the ball it felt like a bomb hit Candlestick. I didn't see the catch, but silence in my mind had broken and the noise was positive. I knew something good had happened. My stomach was about to explode. My only reaction was to pick myself off the ground and signal touchdown.

I was in never-never land; it was a dazed dream. We were ahead but there was still enough time for the Cowboys to catch us. White went right to work and hit Drew Pearson with a 31-yard pass. Drew's catch put Dallas at our 44. Septien was capable of drilling one from there and pulling out the game. Hell, Danny still had time to get them closer. Shit, I could see our comeback drive going down the drain. But there must have been someone watching over the San Francisco 49ers. With thirty-eight seconds left in the game, Lawrence Pillers sacked White, forcing him to fumble. Jim Stuckey fell on the ball. I was still dazed, maybe a little confused. There was only one thing to do; go goddamn crazy.

As I ran through the tunnel and into the locker room, I couldn't catch my breath. I had been on the field so long in the fourth quarter that I collapsed. Our equipment manager, Chico Norton, revived me, but I wasn't in any condition to celebrate.

I did know one thing: There's still room for the dreamers. We were on our way to the Super Bowl.

Although there are two weeks between the NFC Championship and the Super Bowl, the time flies. Writers sit back and pontificate. They offer theories about why the NFL gives the teams the extra week—two weeks total—to get ready for the game.

They write about the extra week because, most of the time, they have nothing else to write about. They quickly become bored and their backs are up against the wall. It's their belief that the game should be played the week following the conference championship games. What they don't realize is we need the extra week.

It's not needed so much to heal a player's bones. By that time of year everyone is pretty well banged up, but our tolerance for pain has reached a point where no one really cares. If they gave us two months off it wouldn't help anyone heal.

What we need is to come down from the season. We were so physically and emotionally exhausted following the Dallas win, we just needed a couple of weeks of relaxation to clear our heads.

But the bottom line is that the excitement of playing in a Super Bowl erases the pain and blocks out the fatigue. I was running on fumes. I'm talking about total exhaustion. But the damage to my body doesn't compare to the damage to the linemen, running backs, linebackers, and receivers.

I don't know how interior linemen play week after week. For that matter, any player who is hit on nearly every play is lucky to be walking by the time the Super Bowl rolls around. The arms and shoulders of interior linemen are a nasty shade of purple. Get this—those are the bruises that are *healing*. New bruises are somewhere between a hot shade of lipstick and fire-engine red. The bruises and welts run from their wrists up to their necks. We're talking about rainbow-colored skin. I'm not taking pain lightly. It's nasty, disgusting to look at. It's simply bad to the bone.

Running backs have scratches covering their entire bodies. It's not pretty. These people play in a different pain zone than I do. I get pushed around and hit pretty damn hard. But it's nothing compared to the way the Lotts, Craigs, Ayerses, Carters, and Ellisons get worked over. Do you remember in high school when they served roast beef for lunch? The meat, known to the guys at Ringgold High School as "mystery meat," had three different shades: green, pink, and brown. It was the food version of the iridescent pants people were wearing along about that time—you know, Three Mile Island jobs, pants that glow in the dark. That's the color of these players' skin in December and January.

Two weeks' rest? Give me a break!

Despite the pain and the fact that the game was being played in Pontiac, Michigan—not exactly your tropical paradise—we were ready for the Super Bowl. The 49ers were so hyped up that Bill believed he had to devise a strategy to calm us down.

There is nothing as berserk as the buildup to the Super Bowl. Although we had never tasted it, we had heard all about it. It's the media at its wildest. Everyone is trying to come up with a unique story in an atmosphere where the news is completely controlled by the NFL. Reporters ask the same questions.

For me, things were nuts. My picture was on the cover of *Time* magazine, and I felt so strange. It made me think of a movie someone told me about. Dustin Hoffman played Harry Kellerman, a reclusive rock star who lived in New York City. One morning Kellerman walked out of his apartment to buy a newspaper and he saw his face on the cover of *Time*. He was excited, but at the same time puzzled. When I saw my face on the cover of *Time* I was excited but wondered what I was doing there. *Time* means current events, presidents and politics, not quarterbacks. Appearing on the cover of a sports magazine is no big deal; they need you to sell magazines and you need them early in your career for the ego trip. But seeing myself on a cover where the pope had appeared was incongruous to me. As former Oakland Raider coach John Madden says: "Hey, wait a minute. What the hell is going on here!" I saw the cover, it shocked me, and I forgot about it. It really wasn't that big a deal.

The championship was what I wanted.

Cincinnati worried me. They did a lot of things defensively that confused me. I was also nervous. This was my first Super Bowl.

The transition from high school to college, and college to the pros was one thing. This was something that was totally different. It was like being in another galaxy, a never-never land. The whole country would be watching a football game. Any thoughts of business or individual problems would play second fiddle to a bunch of guys beating up on each other for one day. Maybe this tells us something about our country.

Hell, why am I philosophizing? But it does make you think.

Despite all the hype, I knew when I went on the field and got hit it would become just another football game. It just was that everything surrounding the game was insane. Bill realized this and created a relaxed atmosphere. We didn't take ourselves too seriously.

When we arrived at our hotel I was met by a graying bell-boy who tried to latch on to my bag. He was persistent. I didn't want to give him my bag; he pulled, I pushed. When I studied the guy's face, I realized it was Bill. He had succeeded in loosening us up even before we checked into the hotel.

When we went to practice in the Silverdome, Bill had music playing. This wasn't only designed to get us used to the acoustics in the dome but to help relax us.

Our PR staff handled the press really well. We had only one session each day with reporters. However, this didn't stop them from asking the same questions over and over again. I couldn't blame the thundering herd of cameras and note pads. It's next to impossible for them to come up with a fresh story. The sportswriters are basically writing the same thing day after day. "Joe, how are you going to attack their defense? Can your running game do the job? By the way, what's your favorite color?" Get the picture?

All this isn't much fun, but I'm not complaining. I'd rather be at the Super Bowl than watching it at home with friends.

What I found to be the key to playing in the Super Bowl, or any important game, is to simulate the way I do things when I'm playing a home game. Keeping this in mind, my mental state remains consistent. By the time a team reaches the Super Bowl, being mentally sharp is more important than the physical stuff. During the first week of practice we put on the pads and hit. The second week is all about the head.

Thinking about what you're going to do is crucial. What I

started gearing my mind toward was how my arm was going to be working. How would I execute? Was I going to have the touch that would put us over the top? I worried about one thing in particular: experiencing a football nightmare, a day where everything could go wrong. Would I fumble the snap from center, trip over the ball, and kick it to a defensive lineman?

I thought about this over and over again. I tried to make myself have a bad dream on purpose. I tried to prevent a football disaster by telling myself that I was going to make mistakes but that my mission was to avoid the big mistake at all costs. Teams go mistake-free and suddenly cough up the ball or break down in a crucial situation.

My plan was not to give up the big interception, the stupid fumble, or the big sack that would turn the game around. If we had to punt the ball away, so be it. There was no way I was going to put our defense in a desperate situation.

I was nervous when I ran onto the field. I knew that all my accomplishments during the regular season would mean nothing if we didn't win. This weighed on my mind. I wanted to win to gain respect and I wanted to make Mom and Dad proud of me.

The noise was deafening. It was crystal clear, like wearing headphones. I could distinctly hear one side of the field and the other side. It was true sound separation. The Silverdome's fabric roof is supported by air pressure. This is why the noise is intense and doesn't drift away.

All this left my mind when we got off to a bad start. Amos Lawrence fumbled the opening kickoff for us on our own 26-yard line and John Simmons recovered for Cincy. Kenny Anderson moved the Bengals to the 5-yard line and it looked like our bubble had burst. Our "D" (defense) got real tough and sacked Kenny at the 11-yard line. This was the first of five times he was brought down behind the line of scrimmage. Kenny was now faced with a third-down pass from the 11-yard line. He dropped back, looking for Isaac Curtis, but his pass was intercepted by Dwight Hicks, who ran it back 27 yards to our 32-yard line.

We were back in business. It was time to pull out our bag of tricks. We have over one hundred passing plays to choose from, and when we go over them I never think they will work. But when we hit the field somehow they usually do. Bill called for the flea flicker. I ran up to the line, took the snap, faked a hand-off, then gave the ball to Ricky Patton. He was running toward the sideline and shuffled the ball to Freddie Solomon, who was cutting the other way. Casper then pitched the ball back to me and I hit our tight end, Charle Young, for a 14-yard gain. The flea flicker caught the Bengals by surprise, and we drove to the 1-yard line. I dove into the end zone for the first score. Moe's extra-point attempt was perfect and we were up 7–0.

In the second quarter we drove 92 yards for a touchdown. It was the longest drive in Super Bowl history, surpassing my buddies, the Dallas Cowboys' 89-yard drive against Pittsburgh in Super Bowl XIII. Our drive took twelve plays, ending in an 11-yard pass to Earl Cooper. Suddenly we were up 14–0.

When we got the ball the next time, Moe kicked a 22-yard field goal, putting us up 17–0. We caught a break when Archie Griffin fumbled the kickoff and Milt McColl recovered at the Bengals' 4-yard line. Moe's two field goals came within thirteen seconds of each other. They were the fastest scores in Super Bowl history. When we went into the locker room at halftime we were leading 20–0. Bill said we still needed 10 points to clinch the win. He wasn't satisfied with a 20–0 lead.

I thought we should play conservatively in the second half to try to avoid a major mistake. The 49ers are a ball-control team, and that's what we were trying to do, just stay in our game plan. Why start running scared? Although the Bengals' defense was playing well, there was no reason for us to panic and change anything we were doing.

Cincy came out smoking in the third quarter. Anderson took his team on a long drive and slid head first into the end zone from 5 yards out. Suddenly it was 20–7. But in the third quarter, the game turned around. The Bengals drove to our 1-yard line and were in a position to cut our lead to 20–14. On fourth down, their fullback big Pete Johnson crashed into Hacksaw Reynolds.

Hacksaw met him quickly. It was the clash of the titans, God-zilla against King Kong. Pete is so big that it's almost impossible to bring him down. Our linebacker Dan Bunz stuck his helmet into Pete, helping to save the day. Bunz had stopped running back Charles Alexander at the 1-yard line on third down after Alexander caught Anderson's sideline pass. The Bengals had three shots at scoring and couldn't push it in. The momentum had returned to the 49ers.

I think we were able to stop the Bengals because our defensive coordinator at the time, Chuck Studley, changed the defensive alignment to key on Johnson, a man who had rushed for 1,000 yards that season. What Chuck did was change the spacing of the defensive line and use a linebacker shooting through to stop Johnson.

The Bengals wouldn't quit. In the fourth quarter, Kenny directed a scoring drive that ended with a 4-yard pass to Dan Ross, making the score 20–14. Moe then hit a 40-yard field goal for us, bringing the score to 23–14. On the Bengals' next drive, Eric Wright intercepted an Anderson pass. This led to another field goal by Moe and gave us a 26–21 game.

This is how it ended. Our season was over and we were the champs. I won it for Mom and Dad.

Mom and Dad:
Things I Should
Have Said

The steps in front of our house in Mon City, as we call Monongahela, must have one big impression from my butt. I spent a lot of time sitting on those steps when I came home from elementary school, waiting for Dad to come home from his job at the Civic Finance Company. I always passed the time holding some kind of ball in my hands. I'd read that Oscar Robertson, the star of the old Cincinnati Royals of the NBA, always dribbled a basketball back and forth from school. He said it really helped him during his college and professional career. When Dad arrived home from work he would be dead tired, but he would always take time to play with me. He saw something in me. At an early age all I wanted to do was play and was enthusiastic about any kind of game. He recognized that my love of sports was above average.

Dad played baseball in the Navy and still loves to play softball. I never asked him, but he is so sports-minded that he might be living his dream, his sports fantasy, through me. Because this may be true, I always think about Mom and Dad whenever I step on the field.

I'm real quiet until I get to know someone, and Dad's the same way. But once he does he's always teasing. I think he's a big kid at heart. When he got home, we would go next door to the Polonolis' to work out in their back yard. They had a tire swing that Dad would move back and forth. To develop accuracy, I would try to throw the football through the center of the tire. Then Dad would run some pass patterns. We ended our football time playing catch and talking about what we did that day.

Many times we would come home and stop in an alley between our house and the Polonolis'. There's a little shed there. Dad would get out his catcher's mitt, lean against that shed, and I would pitch to him. Our relationship was spontaneous. It was beautiful. To this day I don't know if Dad planned any of it. We would go to the basketball court and play one-on-one. If there was a pickup game going on he would play. If he didn't play he would watch. We had an all-sports relationship and didn't talk about much of anything else.

I started playing organized sports when I was eight years old. Dad got me into a peewee football league. My team was called the Monongahela Little Wildcats. The funny thing was kids weren't supposed to begin playing in the league until they were nine. Some way Dad got me in. It was organized sports for me all year round: football in the fall, basketball in the winter, and baseball in the spring. Back then I loved practice, and there wasn't any sport—including football—that I loved more than basketball, because everyone on the court has total involvement. If you didn't have the ball you were in constant motion. It's a game within a game. It's like tag. You have to be moving all the time. I loved dodging, faking, and feinting. The challenge is trying to beat the man who is guarding you.

Up until high school there was no organized basketball in school, so Dad reached into his pocket for the money to rent this little gym. He paid the janitor to take care of the building when we were there. The kids all chipped in—about two bucks each—to pay him back. Dad would get his friends, who were basketball fanatics, to drill the kids on fundamentals. They would set up chairs and we would dribble in, out, and around them. During my junior-high years Dad set up a team. He would drive me and my buddies to different tournaments. Once, we went from a tournament in Bethel Park, Pennsylvania, up to Niagara Falls, New York, where we played a game, then drove all night back to Bethel Park for a championship game in the tournament we were playing there. Even before junior high I was playing sports constantly, and there was a period where I experienced kiddie burnout. When I saw kids involved in non-sports activities, I was a little jealous. I wanted to get off the field.

When I was ten years old I wanted to quit football and join the Cub Scouts. I had finally grown tired of practicing. Our football team had already been practicing for a few weeks when I approached Dad cautiously. I was absolutely certain that he wouldn't be happy with me pulling out after the season started.

"Dad, I want to quit football, I'm tired of it. I want to join the Cub Scouts."

"Joe," he said, "go ahead and quit." But he wasn't going to let me make a mistake at that age. A couple of days later he issued his edict on quitting. "If you want to quit, you can," he said. "But only after you finish playing out the year. I don't want you ever to quit anything you've already started." His message was clear. I finished the season and returned to play the following year. No Cubbies for me.

I guess I was just going through a phase. I wonder if some of the other fine quarterbacks from western Pennsylvania had their Cub Scout phase. Did Dan Marino, Joe Namath, John Unitas, or George Blanda want to join the Cub Scouts? Were the Cub Scouts in existence when Blanda was a kid? People wonder why so many great quarterbacks come from western Pennsylvania. I offer no theories, just an opinion. There isn't a heck of a lot to do when you're a kid growing up there except to get involved in sports. You also play football under terrible weather conditions. The game is played in bitter cold: snow, wind, ice, and sleet. If a quarterback can throw the ball accurately into the teeth of a snowstorm, imagine how he can throw the ball under ideal conditions.

When football is over, the kids play basketball, a game that develops your reflexes. It makes you understand just how important movement and motion are. Fluidity and grace are two really important qualities for a quarterback to have.

Also, by playing sports seriously all year round, you develop a single-mindedness, a sense of purpose. The goals are there for you; there's not much guesswork involved. It's a step-by-step, game-by-game thing. You become conditioned to win.

There's another reason. The people are damn tough. I'm not a fighter. I never was and never will be. But like most people, I can remember the fights I was in as a youngster—all three of them. I had an outrageous temper; when it took hold, I could really get crazy.

One fight I remember began during basketball practice at Ringgold High. Ringgold formed as a result of desegregation. It was a combination of Denora High School—a school that was 50 percent black, and the school I attended, Monongahela, which was predominantly white. Ringgold may have been a combination of two schools, but our gym was of shoe-box proportions. How small was it? It was so small that it looked like a padded cell at Alcatraz. There were tumbling mats hanging all over the walls to cushion the players who were knocked into them.

There was this guy Chuckie, who came from Denora. He was a basketball player, and a real hothead. He would put his head down and bulldoze his way to the hoop. I came to practice one day in a real bad—I mean super terrible—mood. Chuckie went right to work on me. He had no intention of waiting one second before putting my head through one of the mats that covered the gym wall. I went in to lay-up the ball and he knocked me into the wall for no apparent reason.

OK, Chuckie, Joey can dish it out too.

I was in no mood to put up with his shit. As soon as he got

his hands on the ball he drove toward the basket. I purposely put his ass into the wall. I wanted to hurt Chuckie. He got up and ran after me.

"Chuckie," I screamed. "Get out of my face." I was so incensed that I lost my temper and punched Chuckie in the face, knocking him to the floor. The scary thing was that I was so mad, so out of it, I didn't remember punching Chuckie. The next thing I knew, the coach was calling off practice.

While I was dressing, Chuckie came running into the locker room carrying a big piece of wood. It looked like one of those clubs Fred Flintstone carried around. Chuckie's mission was simple: He wanted to wrap that piece of wood around my head. I went on the offensive.

"Chuckie, if you hit me you better make damn sure you kill me. If you don't, I'm going to kill you." I closed my eyes and prepared to die. But to my amazement, Chuckie dropped the club. As Rocky Graziano said: "Somebody up there likes me." Well, maybe I do look insane when I lose it. Whatever, I think that was the last fight I ever had.

Even at Notre Dame, I would enter dunking contests. Yes, this blue-eyed blonde had his own repertoire of dunk shots. I would go up against players on the Notre Dame varsity like Duck Williams, and do my thing. My specialties were the reverse two-hand jam and a dunk where I would bounce the ball off the backboard, catch it, and stuff it through the hoop.

At one point during high school, Dad believed I was going to give up football and accept a basketball scholarship to North Carolina State University. We were driving in the car and talking about schools. He was talking Notre Dame and I was in a rotten mood. "What does all this talk about schools matter?" I said. "I know where I'm going anyway." That was probably my best John McEnroe imitation.

"Yeah," he said. "You probably are going to take the easy way out and play basketball."

That's as close as he ever came to saying he wanted me to play football at Notre Dame. Dad never came out and said it but I knew that's what he wanted. After thinking about it, I knew he was right. Basketball was fun, but in reality there was no future in it for me. I wasn't the right size—I now stand six feet two—and I was certain that if I did play basketball, college ball was as far as I would go.

While all this was going on, Mom, in her own way, was providing me with a lot of strength. She spent a great deal of time alone, and I guess there were times when not having us around weighed on her mind. This might have bothered another woman, but Theresa Montana is an extraordinary person. She got so much pleasure seeing my dad's joy at his son becoming an athlete that I believe it blunted any loneliness she felt. She was happy for him and knew the enjoyment he got out of being with me. We're a close-knit family. When Dad and I finished practicing, we came home and maybe, if we were lucky, Mom would make us some of her famous meat ravioli. Then we would play cards, usually Hearts. We always had a lot of fun. Because I was so outgoing at home, my parents couldn't understand why I was so shy around other people. They didn't worry about it, they just wondered.

Mom is feisty. Sometimes Dad has to hold her when she thinks I'm getting roughed up. If he didn't put a bear hug on her she would run down on the field and throw a few punches at one of those big defensive linemen. You know, she would probably scare the hell out of them.

Mom speaks her piece. During junior high, Dad and I wanted to spend a summer vacation in Canada. Mom didn't. It would have been the second straight year we ventured to the north country. Anyway, we won out. Even though she hated the idea, she reluctantly agreed because she liked it when we were together. We always ended up having a lot of fun. However, when we arrived in Canada, Mom was complaining about everything. We saw snakes and she complained. Snakes never bothered her before. She wanted to go home the minute we got there. Besides the snakes, the weather was damp and overcast. This only added to her bad mood.

It's all smiles for Dad and me following a 1981 win over Atlanta at Candlestick Park.

Talking to the offense early in the fourth quarter of the 49ers' key 17–14 win over Pittsburgh in 1981

Halftime of the "Catch" game against Dallas in the '82 NFC Championship. We were not outhit during that miracle season.

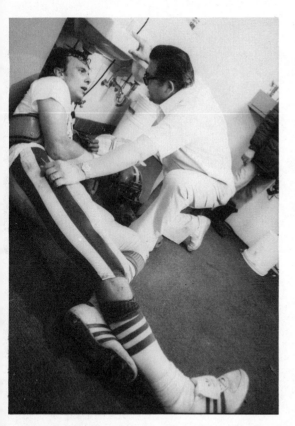

I wasn't doing much celebrating after the 28–27 Championship win over Dallas. Our equipment man, Chico Norton, comforts me after I passed out following the game.

Montana friends and family at Super Bowl XVI. *Left to right*, that's Great Aunt Eleanor; Grandma Josephine in the sweatshirt; Mom; Uncle Sam; Larry Muno, my agent; his wife, Cathy.

On the phone and, freezing in Chicago during a 1983 loss to the Bears. Dwight Clark and Renaldo Nehemiah are close to the heater while Niners' security man Jim Warren looks comfortable in the coat and hat.

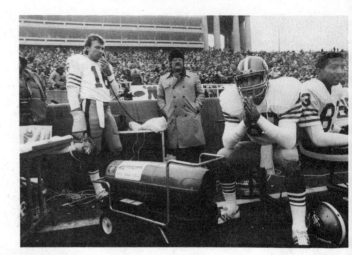

E.T., phone home.... Excuse me. Pointing to the top of the Superdome and feeling on top of the world after throwing two touchdown passes in a 35–3 win against New Orleans, clinching the NFC West Championship in 1984.

Quarterback coach Paul Hackett has a few words of wisdom during halftime of our 51–7 win over Minnesota in 1984. John Ayers (68) surveys the locker-room scene while Matt Cavanaugh studies the Polaroid pictures of the Vikings defense.

Not today, Jim Burt. Getting maximum protection from Randy Cross and Fred Quillan during our 21–0 win against the Giants in the '84 playoffs.

Perusing the Polaroids during halftime of the '84 Giants playoff

Bill Walsh anticipates a victory as the clock winds down against Chicago in the 1984 NFC Championship game.

Media crunch during media day prior to Super Bowl XIX against Miami

Ronnie Lott shares a hand and a smile moments before time runs out on Chicago in the '84 NFC Championship game.

Studying the script with Matt minutes before meeting the Dolphins in the Super Bowl

Getting ready with Dwight Clark in Anaheim before beating the Rams 28–14 during the '85 season

Meditating with Bemular, the Niners' mystical unifying energy force, in Washington before going out and beating the Skins 35–8 in '85

The good-looking one is Jennifer Montana.

Anyway, we were out in the boat fishing and Mom was bitching because she was getting snags in her line and losing her bait. She was also getting really tired and bored with the whole thing. She was WAY past ready to go home. Then the rains came, further adding to her discomfort.

"See what I mean?" she said. "It's raining. I'm tired, and I've got another snag in my line. Sure, guys, I'm having a real *great* time."

Suddenly there was a tug on her line. Naturally, her line got another snag, and it looked like she would lose whatever she'd hooked. Mom couldn't wind it in. Dad started backing the boat up toward whatever was on her line.

"Oh no, the line's moving," she said. "I've really got something here."

You better believe she caught something: a thirty-inch, twenty-nine-pound northern pike. It was the biggest fish we caught all day. When she reeled the fish into the boat it suddenly stopped raining. No kidding. "Hey, guys, maybe we can stay another day or two. What do you think?" Mom was ready to go as in "stay."

Things weren't always that happy. While I was living at home any hardships I might have experienced really didn't register because I had my family and sports. But as I grew older and my career began taking off, there were negatives. There was no way I was prepared for the spotlight. How can anyone prepare for it? My life situation would not only affect me but it would also threaten my relationship with my parents.

The hardships didn't have to do with material things; they were much more personal. I had to grow up fast and the accelerated pace caused me to make mistakes, mistakes that I regret to this day.

Shortly after our 1982 Super Bowl win over Cincinnati, a Canadian film crew, shooting a documentary on Larry Bird, Wayne Gretzky, Gary Carter, and me asked Dad and me to return to the Polonolis' back yard. The crew wanted me to throw passes to Dad just as I did when we had those workouts. As Dad was going out for a pass the director asked me to make him dive for the ball. I led Dad far enough but I didn't know if he would leave his feet to try to catch the ball or just play it safe. He went all out and bit it real bad. He took a head-first tumble into the grass, but got up laughing.

I shouldn't have questioned whether he would go for it. Both Mom and Dad always tried hard to give me love and make my life rewarding and secure. They always sacrificed for me. We weren't poor, but we lived within the structure of a tight budget. That's one reason my folks pushed me toward sports. They knew the money a professional athlete could make. But it wasn't something they talked about when I was a kid. When I was in high school they saw I had the ability to become a professional athlete. Dad seemed to know earlier than that, maybe in junior high. He knew I could play, but what tipped him off was my enthusiasm and dedication to any sport I participated in.

A lot of colleges were interested in me. When I entered Notre Dame, my parents told me to pursue football and dedicate myself to making it.

Mom and Dad knew what it was like meeting payments. There were times when we lived from check to check. It didn't matter as long as we were all together. There was a lot of love there for me. I always had what I wanted or needed, but I know there were things Mom and Dad wanted for themselves that they had to give up. They didn't want me to live my life that way.

Like most parents, they wanted their child to have a better life. I never gave much thought to the future. We were happy most of the time, surrounded by wonderful friends, sincere folks who are still friends to this day. I remember when someone called up on the telephone, our greeting was and still is "Joe's Bar and Grill." People liked to congregate at our house.

Although my parents realized I had above-average athletic ability, they were realistic. They knew the chances of my making it in pro football were one in a hundred. I showed promise but I wasn't a real big kid with a lot of strong physical attributes. My parents thought my athletic ability would get me a scholarship to college. This was important to them. A college degree could ensure a good life for me. It could open up things that my parents never had a chance to realize. I think I sincerely touched their hearts when I received my diploma from Notre Dame.

Looking back, I remember that Mom and Dad were always there for me with good advice. Unfortunately, I didn't always seek it out.

The biggest regret I have in my life is that I didn't confide in them the first two times I got married. I didn't talk to them until it was too late. Why? Why didn't I go to them? This may sound trite but I guess there were two reasons. I wanted them to know I was old enough to take care of myself. Not coming to them was my way of showing that I knew what I was doing when it came to personal affairs. What a joke that was!

The other reason related to my peers in Monongahela. Most of the kids I hung out with there never had the kind of support I had from my parents. They didn't talk to them about anything like school, sports, or dating. They kept everything inside and did things on their own. I would go to my parents in a second when it came to sports or school. But when it came to girls: never. I was just too embarrassed to do it. It's as simple as that.

That feeling stayed with me right through college and into the pros. Now I know that if I had approached my folks with questions about love and marriage I would have received some straight talk. There's a lot of pressure on an athlete who's playing at a big university and winds up in the pros. But in reality, we are all quite young when all this is going on. People need advice and counseling at that age. The media writes about us as if we are fully matured adults. The fact of the matter is we are still growing up, still boys learning about life. The difference between you and me is that beginning in college I was growing up in fantasy land, trapped in a Candy Land existence.

When I was in the midst of marital problems, I would never

pick up the phone and call my parents. I buried my feelings inside and had no outlet, no way to release them. All through college and through most of my pro career I had a hard time saying no to anyone. I was afraid that if I said no I would hurt people. But I was really only hurting myself. I would walk into a room full of people who had shown up to see me and feel totally alone. I walked around with this feeling in the pit of my stomach for such a long time that I learned to live with a knot in my gut. I knew that my parents must have noticed this in me at an early age. It was something I lived with. I really didn't give it much thought when I was young—I was happy.

But as I got older I wasn't strong enough to battle back and find a solution to the problem. My refuge was the football field. I was totally happy when I was playing.

Even if I had gone to my parents and talked to them about getting married I still might have taken the same course. Each time I thought I knew what I was doing. Football, as I said, was a constant struggle for me at Notre Dame, and I'm not very good at dealing with a multitude of problems at once.

I was married for a second time, to Cass, during my first year with the 49ers. This really hurt my folks, but I didn't realize that until after the '82 Super Bowl. I was aware there was friction between her and Mom and Dad but I never did anything about it. I believed everything would eventually work itself out. Looking back on the situation, I should have confided in my parents. They had absoutely no idea how I was feeling. They believed I was being pushed around and thought I was wrong to let myself get into that position.

Dad's way of showing his disappointment was giving me the silent treatment. It wasn't just his son who'd failed to reach out, but his friend. My parents must have thought I didn't trust them, and this had to hurt. I should have been the one to pick up the phone and open the line of communication. In fact, when I hesitate to call my folks about something now, my wife, Jennifer, picks up the phone and gives me a hint. Dad will call Jen to see how I'm doing. He knows that I won't give him straight talk concerning any injury because I don't want to worry him. I'll cop out and say that an injury is healing just fine or I'm feeling a lot better than I did earlier in the week. I'll tell him it's not serious, I'm OK.

Injuries are nothing to joke about. Touchdown passes and comebacks are no cure for personal problems. They're not alternatives for being open and honest with your family. I didn't look for their help and I paid the price. My parents probably always felt comfortable sharing things with me. They've waited a long time for me to catch up. Mom and Dad, I'm finally catching up. Thanks for waiting.

Union Blues

There were all sorts of rumors about the 49ers after we won the 1982 Super Bowl. Of course there's the standard media cliché: We were fat cats, players who went from being a hungry, tenacious football team to a bunch of fellows who were more concerned about raking in the green that comes with being the champs. The media said money took precedence over playing the game.

That's really a minor factor that makes for good gossip. In reality, not many teams have been able to repeat. The incredible Pittsburgh Steelers were the only team to keep that same championship feeling together. They held relationships intact, and this, in my mind, is the key to having a shot at winning back-to-back titles. In the space of six years, the Steelers won four Super Bowls. There are several reasons why teams can't win back-to-back championships. Number one in my mind is that relationships among players change. Of course another obvious reason is opponents focus in on the defending champ. When they play a Super Bowl champ it's their title game; it's like being involved in a playoff-type atmosphere every week.

Also, the media places the champions in the ultrastratosphere. There is no way a team can maintain that image.

Bill's strategy during our 1982 training camp was to put an emphasis on defending the championship. He worked us harder to make a point. Defend, defend, defend—that's all we heard. His idea might have worked. A lot of teams come off a Super Bowl win having to replace people who have been around awhile and have become a step slower. This wasn't the case with us. We were a fairly young and healthy team. There were two things that prevented the 49ers from winning the Super Bowl again. Both played a major factor in turning a close-knit family into a team that came apart at the seams.

First, but not foremost, were drug rumors that the media jumped on and spread. In their minds we took our Super Bowl paychecks and went to the drugstore. Only one player, Craig Puki, a linebacker, tested positive for drugs, and that was it. But the media made the most out of the story.

However, what really tore the 49ers apart in 1982 didn't have anything to do with drugs. We were a team polarized over the possibility of a players' strike. This is where feelings ran deep. It interfered with football, the threat of a strike weighing heavily on everyone's minds. There were intense feelings on both sides of the issue and it was a nasty situation. The animosity among teammates prevented us from ever regaining the special feeling, the togetherness we'd had during the 1981 season.

I'd like to set the record straight. I'm not a member of the National Football League Players Association, but by no means am I antiunion.

My gripes with the union and its leadership during the strike were twofold. I felt the national leadership was pushing the wrong issue on the players. They were looking for a percentage of the owners' gross revenues tied to a graduated wage scale. They were also looking for a piece of the money the three networks paid the owners for the right to televise our games. In my opinion the union should have taken its stand and fought for free agency. I would have gladly supported a strike and stayed out all season to fight for that. If we had broken the stranglehold the owners have over us we would have achieved a miracle.

When I got a look at the issue the national leadership was pushing—which to my knowledge hasn't been gained in any industry under a collective bargaining agreement—I came to the conclusion that the national leadership was incompetent. They were self-serving, leading the players down a primrose path. Their demands were stupid; not only were they unrealistic, they weren't in the players' best interests.

As the strike closed in on the players I was convinced that Ed Garvey, who at that time was the executive director of the NFLPA, was using the union as a stepping-stone for his entry into politics. He sold the players, my friends, a fantasy. He sold them Garvey's Folly—a notion that the players could actually become partners with the owners.

The owners are united and seem to know what it takes to keep us under their thumbs. NFL commissioner Pete Rozelle has the ability to keep his troops together. Al Davis, the managing general partner of the Los Angeles Raiders, took Rozelle to the hoop when he moved his franchise from Oakland to L.A., but that was one of the few times Rozelle lost a battle. Rozelle is usually able to keep his owners in line when necessary.

There was another option Garvey could have used. It's no secret that people had been talking about bringing antitrust cases against the NFL. Garvey didn't have the guts to take that route. It took the United States Football League to make that move. Whether they win or not will be a long story in itself. If the antitrust issue had been brought to the negotiating table, it definitely would have put the fear of God into the owners.

Maybe Garvey realized what I was thinking all along. Rozelle going head to head with Garvey was like a shark fighting a guppy. The players who supported the union might have been angry with the league, but they were taken in by Garvey. If they'd examined his rhetoric closely, they would have realized he was outclassed.

Much of Garvey's rhetoric did deal with antitrust issues. He told the players the owners engaged in collusion. The players didn't need to hear that; they knew that was a fact of life in the NFL. If Garvey had pursued the antitrust issue in the courts and at the bargaining table along with pursuing free agency, I might have been able to get behind him. Even though I thought he would be outclassed in a negotiation, it's a lot easier pulling for an underdog you agree with and respect.

But I could see the owners wanted it more. In their minds they had to win. Sports is a big business with slim profit margins, and the owners are going to fight tooth and nail to remain in control of the players. Look what happened in baseball for a number of years. The owners allowed free agency and took it on the chin. They're still trying to recoup their losses. Believe me, sports is not all fun and games. It's like any other business. The bottom line is what counts.

The union leadership of the 49ers were confused and felt they had to take a stand whether they agreed with the national leadership's position or not.

When the team was discussing a strike everyone was saying that we should pull together and support a walkout. Hell, why should I have supported something I didn't believe in? I thought we should have fought to dump Garvey and put someone in with guts—a guy like Marvin Miller, who ran the baseball players' union and stuck it to the owners. Miller, or a leader who understood the real issues, would have worked for our best interests.

I realize that some of my teammates were saying, "We know why Montana doesn't want to strike, he's making a million dollars a year, he doesn't want to lose that money."

Baloney.

I look at a guy like Walter Payton, killing himself, taking it to the max. He goes free agent and no one picks him up. Is that fair? The owners, TV commentators, and writers will praise him, but in reality he was done in by the system. He contributed to the Chicago Bears' revenue but never had a chance to test a fair and free market.

I have a great relationship with our owner, Edward DeBartolo, Jr., but I know Mr. DeBartolo would still respect me if I fought for a cause. He treats his players well, but he realizes we have a right to make things better for all players. I have tremendous respect for him. He's not the type of guy who would hold a grudge against any of his players if they waged a fair fight.

I would have rather lost the entire season fighting for something that all the players wanted, instead of something that led to a split, something that half the players wanted and half didn't. Neither side could see the other's point. There was a lot of bad-mouthing going on. When I tried to make my point my own teammates put me down.

When the strike was over, no one forgot what happened. We came out with absolutely nothing. I think about 90 percent of the players lost money. There were grudges and we weren't playing as a team. We weren't working together and people weren't talking to each other. How can you win under those conditions? I never believed it would end up that way. I figured when the strike ended, everyone would forgive and forget. I was wrong. A lot of players' heads weren't into the game. We definitely couldn't regain the feeling we had had the year before.

When I look back on the union situation the incident I remember most was the fright-night mentality of Gene Upshaw, a former member of the Oakland Raiders and the players' president of the union. First of all, it's still a mystery to me how he got elected president. I didn't vote for him. As a matter of fact, I didn't even see a ballot. Upshaw must have thought the intimidating tactics he used as a member of the Raiders defense would work on me. "Montana will find out how important he is to the strike when he finds out that his line won't block for him."

For Gene to resort to this tactic only confirmed what I thought from the beginning: He was running scared. He knew the owners were going to deliver a butt-kicking to the union. Looking back at the history of great union leaders, I didn't see many of them making threats unless they could deliver the goods.

He resorted to taking a cheap shot at me. Even the prounion 49ers felt there was no reason for Gene to come down on me. There was no way our offensive line wasn't going to protect me.

Obviously Upshaw was trying to scare me, but it didn't work. In fact, it only made me angry and I played harder. I guess he thought that Raider intimidation could work off the field. Sorry, Gene, I didn't buy your line. I was solid. I knew what I wanted. And I knew that you were in over your head. The season was ruined for us, but Upshaw didn't have anything to do with it. We simply were divided on the issue and could never regroup. All I hoped was that Upshaw, the players who supported him, and Garvey learned a lesson.

I've been thinking about what I'll do when our next negotiation comes up in 1987. My teammates have already asked me if I would join the union and my answer is no. But this doesn't mean I've made up my mind. I want to see what the issues are going to be. Keith Fahnhorst, our union leader at the time of the 1982 strike, who has since stepped down from the position, is a gentleman I respect tremendously. He does a lot of little things for the team during the season that make things easier for us. He's a leader I can support. He puts the players first.

If Bill is doing something that we don't agree with, Farnie will go to him and discuss it. For example, when we had to make that long trip to play the Giants in the '86 wild card playoff game, Farnie got our flight changed so we could get to New Jersey a bit earlier to relax. This might not sound like much but it meant a lot to the team.

As far as the Upshaw stuff, well, I've let it go. I realize people do dumb things in the heat of the moment and I'm not one to hold a grudge. When the time comes, I'll weigh the issues and make a decision based on how I feel. I just hope Upshaw, who is now the executive director of the union, and the rest of the leaders really think about all of the players this time around and don't take another irrational stand.

Rumors

Don't ever let anyone tell you being in the spotlight, under America's microscope, is fun.

After we won that first Super Bowl, and I was voted MVP, I must admit all the adulation and attention was nice. Also, it opened up a lot of financial opportunities for me that I never believed would happen.

But the downside, the dark side of all the notoriety, is letting go of a normal life. This is a tremendous trade-off, especially for a regular guy who cherishes his peace of mind, the right to be left alone and enjoy life. It's not that I'm complaining about being in the spotlight. It's a fact of life for me, and I'm fortunate to realize the benefits of it. But I'm not comfortable with all the attention. Perhaps I'll never be.

I'm quiet. I like to sit in the boat and fish and think about the world and what makes folks tick. But because I'm quiet some people read me the wrong way. I'm not a snob, I'm just a quiet guy. But I'm also an accommodating fellow. If people treat me the way they want to be treated there's never a problem. I'm not talking about anything unusual, just common courtesy.

It's hard going out to dinner. People will ask for my auto-graph at their convenience. They don't care that they're inter-rupting me to chat or get an autograph just as I'm getting ready to eat. I get hungry too. I just want to eat my hot meal and enjoy some good conversation with my dinner guest. As a mat-ter of fact, I love going out to eat with Jen. It's really relaxing. If someone wants to come over before or after dinner, that's fine.

The meal thing bothers me, but seeing false rumors about myself in gossip columns is where the hurt starts. Here's an ex-ample: Jen and I liked to eat at the Fish Market, a restaurant in San Mateo. We used to go there at least once a week because we felt comfortable. The people who dine there are considerate folks. We thought the assistant manager, who knew us, really cared about us. Well, at least to our faces he did.

One morning I opened the *San Francisco Chronicle* and saw an item in Herb Caen's gossip column. Caen said the people who owned the place really appreciated the 49ers' business there, but was Joe Montana so banged up that he had to park his red Ferrari in the handicapped zone? I would never park in a handicapped zone and I had taken my Ferrari there once. The guy who parked his Ferrari there actually was handicapped and he got his tires slashed after the column came out.

This was a bold-faced lie and it really bothered me. The assistant manager was so nice to me. He seemed to be legiti-mately concerned that I was comfortable when I came into his place. I had to believe that he gave it to Caen. I guess he wanted publicity.

Why did he do it at my expense? Why would he try to hurt me? I didn't understand. I did understand that by going to his place regularly I had helped his business. I thought he liked me. I really wasn't concerned about the people who read Caen's column and said, "Who does Montana think he is!" I was more concerned about why the assistant manager took advantage of me. I'm becoming used to this sort of baloney. All too often it comes with the territory. People who I think like me will try to use me for their own purposes.

Rumors circulate so often that I don't pay much attention to them anymore. They're often started by the press thinking out loud. They pick up tidbits of gossip and spread it to their friends and other members of the media. By the time the rumor gets back to me, it's so fantastic I just leave it alone. I'd go crazy if I tried to deal with everything I hear about myself.

After the first Super Bowl win I was perceived as someone who transcended football. All of a sudden I was a celebrity. But writers were disappointed if I didn't live up to what their definition of a "celebrity" was. They believed I was a bad interview when I was just being myself. But generally my relations with the press have been good. Although I've had my moments, there's no animosity between me and most of the members of the media. Since we won that first Super Bowl my meetings with the press have mostly been group sessions. If someone is doing a major story on me, I'll do a one-on-one. But I prefer group interviews because it's easier than answering the same questions over and over again.

Some reporters seem to get irritated if I don't have opinions on everything. Because my career has been successful, some of them expect me to hold the keys to wisdom. A lot of them want to delve into my personal life and why I have done certain things off the field. When I refuse to talk about personal matters, some writers misinterpret me or take me out of context on purpose. They are determined to write the kinds of stories they had in mind all along, not what came out of the interview. Also, a lot of reporters just don't listen. You can tell the ones who don't listen by the way their stories come out.

Once I thought I was giving a reporter a little insight into my personal life. I told him that the first two times I got married, I didn't do the asking. When the story came out, it said the only time I ever said yes was when Jen asked me to marry her. You can imagine how that went down at home. Jen is the only woman I ever asked to marry me.

In short, I'm taken out of context a hell of a lot. At first, Jennifer didn't believe this happened with regularity. However, besides the marriage mistake, she saw other items in the newspaper, and asked me if I was quoted accurately because the quote didn't sound like me. Jen suggested that we run our own experiment.

Glenn Dickey, a columnist for the *San Francisco Chronicle* who has been quite critical of me in the past, wanted to do a cover story in 1984 for *Inside Sports*. I was skeptical. He said it would be a good way of introducing Jennifer to San Francisco and the nation. OK, I could buy that idea.

Jen taped the interview Dickey did with me and discovered he took a lot of things out of context. Now she knew what I was talking about, and it bothered her a lot because she wasn't used to the sleaze factor. Dickey, in particular, is what I call a hit-and-run artist. He hits and hides, like a phantom.

Sure, *Inside Sports* wanted to introduce Jennifer. Both of us were on the cover, but the headline read: THE COOL DAYS AND HOT NIGHTS OF JOE MONTANA.

I mean, what kind of misrepresentation was that? When I saw the cover I just about died. Jen was really upset, but there was nothing we could do at that point. I hated it just as much as she did.

"Joe, how can they do this? Why would he twist things? Why would he want to hurt us?"

"That's the way it goes," I said. "Just let it go."

I couldn't wait until that particular issue of the magazine was off the newsstand.

There is a way of guarding against this. I'm aware of writers who will try to draw controversy out of me to make them look good. When I'm doing an interview with one of them, I'll prepare. I'll think of what I'm going to say, so they can't twist anything. When I'm actually in the interview, I'll repeat the question and my answer and somehow get the reporter to repeat my answer. If I think someone is out to do a number on me, I'm going to make sure he gets it right. Then if they still do a number, well, at least I know it's fiction. Obviously some editors don't care about checking their reporters' facts or methods. But who am I to change sports journalism?

I'm accustomed to being quoted out of context. In fact I rarely read the sports section of the papers during football season. I look at headlines and skim the paper. The only time I read a story in its entirety is when another player suggests that I do. This isn't just the results of experiences I've had. When Renaldo Nehemiah, the world-class track man from the University of Maryland, came to the 49ers I had preconceived notions about him. The stories I read about "Skeets" painted a picture of a cocky egotist who believed he was going to become an instant starter. When I met him, he was the direct opposite of the man portrayed in the press. He wasn't any more cocky or confident than anyone else on the team.

During the '84 season, while the 49ers were on their way to one of the greatest seasons in NFL history, the San Francisco press seemed to be looking for ways to tear the team apart. Even during that first Super Bowl year, they were conditioned to losing. As we won game after game, they still were skeptical. I'm not thrilled with criticism that is unwarranted, but it goes with the territory.

Our performance on the field is fair game. But even there, there were some downright cheap shots. A master of the low blow is Lowell Cohen, a writer for the *San Francisco Chronicle*. He says he only likes being around the 49ers when they lose. In fact, he wrote that he enjoyed coming into our locker room when we lost our opening game against the Minnesota Vikings in 1985. He also expressed joy at our loss to Denver in '85, during which a fan threw a snowball at Matt Cavanaugh, who was holding for Moe Wersching as he was attempting a field goal. The snowball was no excuse for a loss, he wrote. Well, no one on the team ever offered it as an excuse for losing the game.

I have no respect for a person like Cohen, who enjoys kicking us when we're down and does it for a living. He has absolutely no credibility, as far as I'm concerned. He's only interested in hurting folks to bolster his reputation. I don't spend a lot of time figuring out his motives. I just feel sorry for him.

The other thing that bothers me is the timing of stories. When something breaks concerning a player or situation involving the team, that's one thing. But it seems funny that certain writers pen the same story at the same time each year.

A couple of days before the season begins each year, Ira Miller, of the *Chronicle*, prints his annual 49ers salary-information story. Ira's been covering the 49ers for almost ten years; he seems to be a sensitive and caring gentleman. But Ira knows damn well that salary information is going to bother some people. He has a right to print whatever he wants, but I wonder why he does it right before the season starts.

It's not Ira's job to help the team. In fact, his role is adversarial. But printing the salary information at a time he knows it is definitely going to affect us negatively is damn selfish and petty on his part. Ira can also get downright nasty. Before our wild card playoff game in 1985 with the New York Giants, he asked me if I thought Giants quarterback Phil Simms was overconfident and cocky. I know Ira knows better. If I had said yes on the record I would have given Simms even more reason to want to beat us. So Ira took an off-the-record comment out of context and printed it.

I told Bill Verigan of the New York *Daily News* that asking a question like that before a playoff game was like asking someone if he had stopped beating his wife. The whole thing upset me. That's just not my style and anyone who knows me realizes that.

To add insult to injury, Ira also said that I would have voted for Bears quarterback Jim McMahon over Simms for the Pro Bowl. The fact is I don't care who the quarterback is in the Pro Bowl. Sure, it's nice to be voted into the game; it shows that your peers respect you. But I don't even vote for offensive players; defense votes for offense and offense votes for defense. Ira knows this. As far as Simms goes, I didn't pay any attention to him during the season. I have enough to do without studying the stats of other players.

Ira hit me with a cheap shot and I'll have a hard time talking to him again. I sincerely thought he had more class than to pull a stunt like that. He's a respected writer, but now I've got to wonder what his motives really are. The incident surprised me. I remember a wonderful conversation I had with Ira on a flight from San Francisco to the 1985 Pro Bowl in Hawaii following our win over Miami in Super Bowl XIX. Reflecting on that talk, I just don't understand why he brought up the Simms thing.

When push comes to shove, I can handle the way the press has treated me and the 49ers. I'll sit down and talk to any reporter. They may not get the information they want but I will give them a shot. If I don't feel like talking, I'll let them know. In 1985 I was so disgusted with the *San Francisco Chronicle's* coverage of me and the 49ers I stopped talking to its reporters. Maybe that's why Ira went after me.

These differences with the media are discomforting. I'd like to have a decent relationship with these guys because I'd enjoy sitting down and sharing stories and shooting the breeze with them. It would be relaxing for all of us.

The rumor mill is fueled by the media, and when they take aim at my personal life I get furious. That was the case during the '85 season, when rumors spread about me using drugs. I'm not going to point the finger at anyone for starting these rumors. They were bold-faced lies. Anyone who knows me and anyone I care about knows that.

Drug rumors hit the 49ers early in the 1982 season after we won our first Super Bowl. It was then I began realizing that media gossip can be just as harmful as a story that gets into print. All someone has to do is insinuate that someone is using drugs and it becomes unpleasant. You have to watch everything you do in public. I stopped going to the bathroom in restaurants during the '82 season because I knew people were watching and that some would be saying: "He's gone to the bathroom twice. He must be doing cocaine or something." Sounds stupid, right? Wrong.

I found out that people automatically assume things about people who are "blessed" to be in the limelight.

Since 1982 the issue of drugs and sports has been brought into the open. Some athletes have admitted they are users and gone for treatment. Others have been convicted of selling and possession.

This has led to another phenomenon. If a team isn't playing well, the press and fans can always say, "Oh, you know why so-and-so had such a rotten day." Drugs now seems to be the all-encompassing reason for a player or his team's poor performance. No one can convince me this is the case in any other field of endeavor. If a stockbroker makes a few bad suggestions in a row, do you blame it on drugs? If a doctor is sued for malpractice, should we blame it on drugs?

Yes, I know those people aren't so-called celebrities. But let's look at celebrities a minute. If an actor gives a terrible performance, does the audience stand up in the theater, boo, and call him a drug addict? Do the critics write: "Well, you know why Mr. Actor was bad in this film. Don't you?"

The answer is no. When an athlete doesn't meet the public's expectation nowadays, drugs are usually perceived to be the reason. If they can't blame it on injuries, if they can't blame it on the coaching staff or the front office, both the public and media feel comfortable blaming in on drugs. I know all about this because it happened to me. The 1985 season started poorly for me. Before I reported to training camp my back was bothering me and continued to get worse as camp progressed. When we started the season it still was bothering me.

It didn't help my performance. Besides my back problem, I also knew the 49ers were in a no-win position. We couldn't possibly duplicate our 1984 season, when we'd gone 18-1 and beaten the Miami Dolphins in the Super Bowl.

The theme during training camp was how difficult it is to repeat as champions. We had found out just how difficult during the '82 season, when we had a hard time winning. Maybe all this talk put us in a negative mind-set—who knows? When we began struggling I became the focal point of the team's problems.

If I hadn't played on two Super Bowl winners perhaps I

wouldn't have been judged so harshly. During the early part of the season I was up among the leading quarterbacks in terms of statistics. People said I was throwing too many interceptions. In one game I threw four. Two balls were tipped and intercepted and one was a desperate pass that I put up for grabs in the end zone. There were also complaints that my yardage per passing attempt was too low. But my yards per completion were up over '84. Then of course there was the old standard theory that I just couldn't throw the long ball. Well, I popped a few deep passes that were either dropped or called back because of penalties.

Except in the game against the Chicago Bears, we were in a position to win all the early season games we lost in the last couple of minutes, but just didn't pull it out. Sometimes it was me, sometimes it was the plays Bill called, sometimes we fumbled, sometimes I threw the ball away, and sometimes our defense had a bad day. Things weren't going perfectly, as they had in '84.

There are no certainties in football. Maybe that's why the ball is shaped the way it is. It can bounce to you or bounce away. The sports reporters who were paid to analyze "what's wrong with the 49ers" couldn't do it. That's when they started speculating among themselves. When nothing makes sense to them I guess there's only one thing to assume: The quarterback is on drugs.

It seems since 1982 some writers have tried to analyze my quiet nature or my personality or whatever. In pursuit of evidence for their analysis, I think some of the media tend to look for things to pin on me. I'm not blaming them for starting the drug rumors in '85 because I don't know where they began. One thing I do know is that they began early in the season.

Bill began calling my agent, Larry Muno, after the second or third game in the season, asking him if I was OK and if he had heard any of the same rumors he had been hearing. One had me stopped in Monterey for driving a hundred miles per hour in my Ferrari. The way that story goes is when the police stopped me they found an ounce or a gram of cocaine or whatever in my car. Another one had me drunk in Atlanta and in possession of drugs. In this tale Willie Brown, a California state representative, called the mayor of Atlanta, who supposedly got me out of trouble. I was also supposed to have been seen doing drugs the night before our game with the Detroit Lions in Pontiac.

It got crazier. People said I was checked into a drug-treatment center by Wayne Walker's doctor. Wayne is a former Detroit Lions linebacker, now a sportscaster in San Francisco. Then there was the familiar line that I was seen enjoying cocaine in the back room of a famous restaurant.

Not only was Bill calling Larry but a lot of reporters were also calling him to see if he knew anything about these rumors. Reporters started asking me about them, and all I could say was there was no truth to the rumors. As long as the rumors were confined to guys inside the media, I didn't worry too much about them. But the stories began to spread.

They seemed to be moving around the country. Frank Cooney, a sportswriter for the *San Francisco Examiner*, told me that Paul Zimmerman from *Sports Illustrated* asked him what he knew about the rumors. I could sense things were getting out of hand. I went to Bill and told him these rumors weren't true and I didn't know what to do about them. He was nonchalant and told me not to worry about the situation. In reality, he was extremely worried, but for some reason he didn't let on to me.

It didn't take him long to change his mind. He called me back and said that maybe the best thing we could do, if we got the chance, was to go public with the whole thing.

"I don't know about that," I said.

"There would be some good and some bad in bringing it before the public," Bill said. "Maybe we could get the whole thing defused faster." Then he asked me about specific rumors.

"No, nothing happened in Atlanta. The only time I left the hotel was when I went to dinner with the linemen," I said. "That took about an hour or two. I took a cab to the restaurant and came back in one. In Detroit the only time I left my room was to eat dinner alone in the hotel restaurant.

"As far as being stopped in the car in Monterey, what kind of car are they saying I drove?" I asked.

"The Ferrari," Bill said.

"Well I haven't had the Ferrari in San Francisco all season. It's been in L.A. since I left for training camp."

"Joe, have you ever been stopped, just stopped? Forget about being pulled over for drinking or drugs. Have you ever been stopped by the police anywhere?"

"No. I've never been stopped anywhere."

This didn't register in my mind as any great confrontation between Bill and me. Perhaps if it had come out of the blue it would have angered me. But at the time, I had to get this off my chest, I wanted someone to believe me. I wanted someone on the team to stand behind me. I may have cleared the air with Bill but things were getting worse.

Riki Ellison, our linebacker, came to me and said that one of his neighbors was approached by a reporter who repeated some of the rumors and wanted to know if he knew anything about them.

Randy Cross came and told me that Charlie Bricker, a reporter for the *San Jose Mercury* and the king of the gossips, tried to put him on the spot.

"Where was Joe between nine and nine-thirty the night before the Chicago game?" He asked.

"He was in a meeting," Randy said.

"Yeah, but are you sure?" Bricker asked.

"Hell yes, I'm sure he was there, because I was there. We always look at film at that time before a game."

By now there were too many people, outside of the normal gossips who usually spread this kind of thing, talking about me. The stories were growing and getting embellished. It was football's version of the kid's game "Telephone." Only this wasn't funny. These people were messing with my life and my family's well-being.

Normally when a problem occurs I can separate myself temporarily for practice or a game, but this was different. These rumors bothered me to the extent that although they weren't preoccupying me when I was playing, they were like a nagging toothache that just wouldn't go away.

Through all this, my teammates, understandably, were reluctant to say anything to me or anyone else about it. Some of them tried to help but they couldn't get too involved. This didn't bother me because I know we're operating in a strange climate in pro sports today.

These rumors put a cloud over my head, and anyone who voluntarily aligned himself with me would have likely become a target. If a teammate was questioned about something concerning me he could directly answer, he would. But other than those instances, no one went out of his way to help me. I didn't feel abandoned because no one really wants to get near a drug problem—even if it's a false rumor. Obviously, I couldn't let things continue the way they were.

Jennifer was strong through the whole thing, and I knew my parents had heard and been approached about the stories. They didn't call me on it. They knew it wasn't true.

I knew some reporters were talking behind my back. John Rochmis, from the Oakland *Tribune*, who was NOT one of the guilty ones, caught me on a real bad day. I had just been questioned by a few reporters who confronted me with other rumors. John said his piece and I came down on him.

"I'm going to tell you what I told the rest of them. I'm starting to feel like that guy who was accused of rape, went to prison, and years later the girl says she lied about him. Go ahead and print what you want. The only satisfaction I can get out of anything you might print is to take legal action. You're just going to have to take your chances.

"What you're about to print isn't true. It's going to be damaging to me and you know you can't prove any of these rumors. I'm going to do what I have to do to protect myself and my family. If you want to print what you think is the truth, go right ahead."

I knew I lost my temper. I don't think I ever came down on

a reporter like that before, but I was mad. I felt sorry for Rochmis. During training camp his editor assigned him some baloney story that was supposed to be called "Joe Montana: The Untold Story." He said he wanted two hours and I said I would give him a half hour. Did he think I was going to sit still for a story like that? I gave him about a half hour's worth of one-word answers. It wasn't a pleasant experience for me and I don't think he enjoyed it either.

Shortly after that November interview with Rochmis, Bill and Larry asked me if I wanted to go public with the rumors. I decided that something had to be done. This could only drag on and the stories would only get more outrageous as time passed. But I wasn't sure what the results of going public would be. Would it really clear the air or would the publicity screw things up even more?

During Bill's press conference, Sam Skinner, a free-lance reporter, asked him about the rumors surrounding me. Bill categorically denied them. He spoke for about eight minutes without any interruption. He said I would be giving my side of the story the following day. I was relieved. The next day when I saw the headlines, I didn't feel too terrific. When I saw my name next to the words "drugs" and "cocaine" it was a real shock to my system.

At my press conference I pointed out that this situation wasn't like someone accusing me of being a late-night barhopper. It was dead serious. I was affected; my family was affected. Someday when she's old enough my daughter is probably going to ask me what happened during this period: Was anything that was said true? My parents had been through a lot with me and now they had something else to worry about. In short, this was my life. I make a lot of money but it's no remedy for this horrible situation. How would anyone feel if people were putting them on trial, and acting as judge and jury?

I wondered why the writers, instead of talking and spreading rumors, didn't try to check things out through other sources. Call the hotels, canvass the police, look for records, find the officers who supposedly pulled me over. I guess that would have been too hard for them to do. Maybe they realized a check would have proved the rumors were false, which would have killed a sellable news story.

After Bill's press conference some of the writers were disgusted with Sam Skinner because he'd brought the issue out in the open; they believed he'd blown any potential stories they might break. How selfish and uncaring can these people be? I guess they wanted the thing to drag out so the rumors could spread further. A good rumor must make their jobs easier because it gives them something to write about in addition to what's happening on the field.

The day after my press conference, Charlie Bricker, the reporter for the *San Jose Mercury,* called Larry up and said he heard I was going to be checked into a hospital for drug rehabilitation in a couple of days. This blew my mind. If he thought this was the case, why didn't he confront me face to face? I shouldn't be surprised at Charlie pulling something like that because he strikes me as being somewhat obtuse and shallow. He asks the same "insightful" question after every game and he must get me alone to do it. "Joe, what was your assessment of the game?"

I don't blame any of the media for looking into the rumors. Some writers even came to me after my press conference and tried to explain why they'd pursued the story. Garry Niver of the *San Mateo Times* and Kevin Doyle of the Palo Alto *Times Tribune* apologized to me. They said they weren't trying to be malicious, they were just doing their job.

They impressed me as a couple of men who understood the seriousness, the personal nature of the whole episode. Believe it or not, some humor emerged. No matter how serious things seem to be with the 49ers, nothing is untouchable when it can be used as part of our locker-room humor. The day after Bill's press conference the story about the whole affair was on the front page of the *Chronicle.* It was right next to a man who had been Rock Hudson's lover and was suing Mr. Hudson's estate because the film star allegedly never told his friend he had AIDS.

Well, during the '85 season our blackboard humor had been reserved for drawing ghosts to get on Freddie's nerves or little catfish, in honor of Roger "Catfish" Craig, our great running back. The day after the news conference, someone cut out the Hudson story and placed my picture on that piece in place of the guy Hudson lived with. Even I had to laugh.

I probably would have joined right in on the fun if the same thing had happened to someone else. It's weird: A lot of things seem funny when they are turned into locker-room jokes. Unfortunately, it's probably the only laugh I got out of the whole mess.

On the surface, my name has been cleared. The support I got from the fans during the weeks following the press conference was tremendous. When we played Kansas City the week the stories hit the papers, the Candlestick crowd greeted me with a tremendous ovation. Many writers from across the country wrote stories and columns supporting me.

But in reality, I expect that if I ever get into a slump again, or play poorly, the rumors will start again. There's no protection because I really didn't know how they got started this time. One theory that went around, and I guess I have to give credence to it, is that the gambling community may have started them. I know for a fact that a tip sheet published in the Boston area ran a story headlined IS MONTANA ON COCAINE? It would be naïve of me to think that football betting is going to disappear, but what bothers me is how the NFL—and rightly so—will crack down on players if they get a whiff of gambling activity but, by its silence, does nothing to discourage football gambling in general.

It would be impossible for the league to do anything about the touts and people who run betting services all over the country; this is not under its jurisdiction. However, the league is in a definite partnership with the networks. By allowing each network to have an in-house tout, it gives tacit approval to betting.

I wonder how NFL executives, who allow this climate to exist, would feel if they had to go through what I did. I know things aren't going to change. But it's possible that I, and perhaps others, have gone through hell because the NFL stands by silently and condones gambling.

I guess I'm supposed to learn to live with all of this but, believe me, I never will. The next time you think you would like to leave what you're doing and trade it for the life of a high-profile athlete, think twice. A player can get used to the highs and lows of winning and losing. Losing isn't fun, but experiencing it and coming to grips with the fact that I can't play perfectly in every game makes the feeling manageable.

Having to deal with lies that I can't do anything about, however, makes me stop and wonder if playing professional football is really enough of a reason to be put through this kind of pain. Even though I have a love affair with football, for the first time in my life I wondered if living for Sunday is actually worth all the sleepless nights I went through.

11

The Man They Call Genius

Guy Benjamin, a backup quarterback during my early years with the 49ers, was a gentleman who marched to the beat of a different drummer. Some people might have characterized Guy as a bit of a flake, but when it came to laying things on the line he didn't mince words.

Guy was brutally honest, even with regard to Bill Walsh, who coached him during his college days at Stanford University. In 1977 Guy Benjamin was an All-American quarterback, and he knew all about the man who strikes the familiar, reflective, Jack Benny hand-on-chin pose on the sidelines, watching his team.

"Joe, no matter how well you play for Bill, don't ever expect to get a game ball or be named a captain," Guy explained to me. "Bill doesn't mean anything by it, he just expects his quarterbacks to play great all the time. Anything less doesn't sit well with him. Bill will accept mistakes from people who play other positions, but not his quarterbacks."

I was familiar with the quarterbacks the press had given Bill credit for developing: Dan Fouts, San Diego's great bearded one; Cincinnati's Kenny Anderson, who I opposed in our first Super Bowl win; Greg Cook, another Bengal, who won an NFL passing title; Sam Wyche, who now coaches the Bengals and was my first quarterback coach with the 49ers; Virgil Carter, yet another Bengal; Guy Benjamin; and Steve Dils.

I knew Bill's reputation, but Guy's words rang in my ears: They were shocking. It was déjà vu. I didn't get credit from Devine until the end of my Notre Dame career, and now I was facing the same situation with Bill.

However, as time passed, I found out Guy wasn't exactly accurate concerning Bill's quarterback philosophy.

During the 49ers' 1984 run at the Super Bowl, Bill selected Matt Cavanaugh as captain before our game with the Philadelphia Eagles. I didn't play during the game because my ribs were torn apart. After the game—which we won—Bill came up to Matt and gave him a hearty pat on the back.

"Matt, you played a heck of a game," Bill said. I was dressing right next to Matt and heard the conversation. Then Bill turned to me. "Oh yeah, Joe, you played OK too," he said in a kidding tone.

I didn't know what to make of his comment, so I took it as a joke. But deep down inside I was hurt. I never gave anything short of 1,000 percent for Bill, and I never received a compliment from him, never a touch of humanity.

All this might sound trivial to you, maybe a little childish. After all, I make a lot of money playing quarterback, so why should I be concerned with getting a little praise from Bill once in a while? But don't you enjoy getting a pat on the back from your boss? Sometimes praise is worth more than the money. It comes from the heart. You know you are respected by the man running the show. I respect Bill as a coach, but as a person on and off the field, he confuses me.

Bill once said that Joe Montana was no Einstein. That hurt but I shook it off. The only way I can rationalize a comment like that is believing Bill doesn't really know me and has no confidence in me. There are things I see happening on the field that I know we can do but I'm reluctant to go to Bill because I know that nine times out of ten he's not going to take my suggestion. He knows how I feel. I remember during one game we weren't moving the ball and I was getting a lot of pressure, forcing me to dump the ball. After one series, I was coming off the field and he let me have it.

"Joe, what the hell are you doing out there, can't you get the job done?" That was it. I knew damn well that the whole team was having a rough day and I was trying my best. He still found it necessary to make me the scapegoat.

"Bill, if you don't like the way I'm playing, pull me out," I yelled. "But don't jump in my face, because it's not going to help anything. You know it and I know it."

He didn't say anything. He just walked away from me. But I know he was surprised because he went to Paul Hackett and told him to find out what was wrong. Bill wanted to settle me down.

I'm not the only player who will second-guess Bill. I'll call one of his plays and someone will ask why we don't run the ball. "Hey, guys, I just work here. You know what I mean," is my usual reply. I try to put these incidents in their proper perspective and let them go. Let's just say these situations become routine. They're not daily occurrences, but things I've learned to live with.

There is one thing I'll always have a hard time understanding. After the 49ers won that first Super Bowl in 1982, Bill did something out of the ordinary. Something that I'll never forget.

The following season was interrupted by a players' strike. The 49ers ended up playing an abbreviated nine-game schedule. We went 3–6 but missed qualifying for the wild card spot by the skin of our teeth. Or should I say by the skin of Moe's foot. During the final game of the season, Moe had a last-second field goal against the Rams blocked. If he'd made it we'd have been in the playoffs. We played our guts out and came up empty.

The day after the Ram game we all got together for a final

team meeting and Bill didn't show. Why didn't he come to the meeting? I can't answer that question because I still don't know. But I'll tell you this: When I think of him pulling a no-show it still bothers me. Not only didn't Bill come to the meeting, he gave everyone the impression that the 49ers were gutless wonders, a team who didn't care about winning it all again during the 1982 season. "They didn't want to win as much as I did," Bill told the press. No one wanted to win that Los Angeles game more than I did, and Bill knew it. He talked a lot during that season about how I was doing too much off-the-field work and how I wasn't concentrating on playing quarterback. That was pure bunk. Football always comes first for me. Any business I had to conduct that was not pertaining to the game was done on my days off.

He compounded his actions during the off-season by keeping the team on the edge of our collective seats, not knowing if he would return as coach. Bill never talked to any of his players during that off-season. This upset me. He just went about his business. Maybe he was confused. Maybe he didn't know what to do. Losing bothers all of us, but that year it really got to Bill. He was under intense pressure. He told people he might retire, that he had had it with the tremendous highs and the sudden, abysmal lows of coaching. Before the 1983 minicamp, Bill went to a number of people to see how he might approach the situation. I talked to other players about what Bill might do. He remained silent but returned as coach.

Maybe Bill thought silence was truly golden. We realized he was going through troubled times. The press, in their own inimitable way, had labeled him a "genius," the man who was coaching's state of the art. Bill had taken a sudden fall from that lofty status and people were ready to tear him down. I felt for him, but he should have confided in his players. After all, we rally around him when our backs are to the wall. I'm sure we would have told him to take it easy, the 49ers would be back. Bill Walsh had trouble living with his fall from the top, but when all was said and done he was able to overcome adversity.

At that particular time, however, he mistreated his players—
people who played to the max, played in pain because, win or
lose, we all believed in Bill. We all also realized that everyone is
entitled to make a mistake. We knew that Bill had suffered his
own kind of pain. He paid tremendous dues to reach the heights
he obtained, and he did it the hard way. He worked his butt off
for everything he got.

Bill began his career in 1957 at Washington Union High
School in Fremont, California. The team had lost twenty-six of
twenty-seven games over three previous seasons before Bill took
over. But during Bill's second season, his methods took hold.
The team went 9-1 and captured the conference championship.

After the high school experience Bill had a number of jobs:
assistant at the University of California; assistant at Stanford;
assistant with the Oakland Raiders, where he began his pro
career in 1966 as Al Davis's offensive backfield coach; an eight-
year term as an assistant with the Cincinnati Bengals; and assistant with the San Diego Chargers.

Finally he got his break in 1977, when he was named
head coach at Stanford University. His hard work had paid
off, but there was always the general feeling that Bill should
have become a professional head coach sooner in his career. He
was overlooked, and I believe this affected him. It molded
his philosophy. Let's face it, he had to feel he was prepared
to be a head coach in the NFL long before he got the San
Francisco job.

From all I've read about Bill's Cincinnati experience, it
must have left a lasting impression on him. He went into the job
with a real chance of becoming head coach of the Bengals. Bill
was working for Paul Brown, the former coach of the Cleveland
Browns and an NFL legend, who apparently was getting ready
to either retire or move into the front office on a full-time basis.
Unfortunately, Bill's job—offensive coordinator—turned out to
be more of a curse than a blessing. I can relate to Bill's situation
with Brown. We're talking about pure jealousy. Bill was trying
hard to make a name for himself, while Paul was hanging on to

his own identity as a legend in the game. This caused friction between the two men. Bill was trying to establish his own reputation, a rep that would land him a head coaching job. From what I've read and heard, the two men ignored each other. The only time they were seen together in public was on the sidelines.

The whole situation bothered Bill. He kept to himself and the players he coached were reclusive. He was disgusted about being Paul's assistant but he couldn't do anything about it. Bill wanted some credit for any success Cincy had and Brown made sure Bill didn't get any.

Brown was also having a rough time. After a Bengal win, he would tell the press about plays the team used that weren't even in the playbook. Bill realized Paul was confused.

In team meetings, Paul would diagram plays with twelve players. In fairness to Paul, Bill was so mad it made him say things he wouldn't normally say. He told reporters that Brown was "filled with poison" and had a "warlike nature."

Bill's an intense fellow and it definitely showed during his days with the Bengals. He's also proud, and that can be a problem when it's carried to an extreme. At one point during his Bengal tenure, Bill said he was a candidate for the Houston Oilers head coaching job. But Paul wouldn't release Bill from his contract. Bill believed that Paul was purposely impeding his career. Finally, after eight troubled years together, Paul decided to call it quits in 1975. Bill Walsh was a free man.

He moved to the San Diego Chargers, but still was an assistant, working as offensive coordinator for former UCLA coach Tommy Prothro. Bill wasn't going to hang out there long. I guess he'd learned his lesson the hard way. Then he finally got the head coaching job he treasured. But it wasn't in the NFL, it was back at Stanford.

He didn't waste any time turning the program around. In 1977, Bill took the Cardinals to their first Bowl appearance in six years. The team finished the season with an 8-3 record and beat LSU 24–14 in the Sun Bowl. Bill was named the Pac-10 coach of the year. The following season, Stanford posted an 8-4 record and came back from a 22-0 deficit to beat Georgia 25–22. Less than two weeks after that win, Bill got the call he had wanted for twenty-one years. Edward DeBartolo, Jr., wanted to turn the 49ers into winners and believed Bill was the fellow to do it.

He offered the coaching job but Bill also wanted to be general manager. After all those years of working for someone else, he wanted complete control of the team.

Initially Mr. DeBartolo balked at the idea, but he realized it was the only way he would get Bill. Nine days after that first phone call, Bill Walsh was named head coach and general manager of the San Francisco 49ers.

It's no secret that Bill is a complex fellow, but one thing that has remained a consistent part of his personality is his sharp sense of humor. When he's on and in a good mood, he always leaves us laughing. I remember one of the first meetings he ever held after he became coach. The subject of the meeting was our dress code for road trips.

Bill came striding into the meeting room dressed as General George Patton. He was followed by some of his coaches, who were dressed in a variety of bizzare outfits. I don't remember who was wearing what except for Bobb McKittrick who resembles Kojak.

"Gentlemen," Bill said, "I want you to listen up. Look at these people—strange, aren't they? You wouldn't want to look like them, would you?" This was Bill's way of telling us how not to dress when we went on a road trip.

Bobb was dressed completely in white with a long smock and beads. Topping off his outfit was a long blond wig. Another coach was dressed completely in plaid. I'm talking about plaid on plaid: plaid pants, plaid shirt, and plaid socks. The fashion show continued with your basic hillbilly look. A coach dressed in bib overalls, no shirt, and no socks.

Bill's pièce de résistance was a coach dressed in a regular pair of pants, a conservative shirt, and a nice pair of shoes. Oh, there was one thing that "stuck out" about this coach's clothes. He had a large salami inside his pants. We all got the meaning.

The more time I spend with Bill the more I realize that everything he teaches, every tactic he employs on a football field, has a great deal of significance. With me it's his famous system. Let's face it, the underlying basis of any friction between Bill and me is his desire for people to believe I am one of the better quarterbacks in the game because of his offensive system. My feeling is that Bill's system and the quarterback work hand in hand. I believe you need the right person to play within the system. Not any quarterback could achieve what I have simply because of a coach's system.

Deep down inside, I think Bill knows that. There are times when I lose my cool in my dealings with Bill, but I've also gained strength while working with him. I'll take negatives and try to turn them into positives. I'll listen to what he says and say to myself, "I don't care what he does or what he says, I'm determined to be the best that I can be." I don't care what Bill or anyone else says, there are things I know I can do on a football field that no one else is capable of doing. No one will ever destroy this feeling, not with words or head games. It's something that has lived inside me for a long time.

Ultimately, I would like to see my relationship with Bill evolve to the point where I become involved in planning some of the offense. Now, I'm not looking for a lot. If I were involved, it would cut down on the number of plays we use in a game. I think that this would help our offense. For example, if we're faced with a third-down play and Bill's not sure of what to do I would like to get the OK to go with my own idea instead of having to recall forty plays to use against a nickel defense or the twenty third-and-3 plays we have in our system.

I think Bill is becoming more receptive to ideas like this. There was one play I brought to him toward the end of the 1985–86 season. It was something about getting a tight end out on a pass pattern in a different direction. Bill gave me a quizzical look and tapped his fingers on my chest. "Maybe that will work," he said. "Maybe that will be better."

He will always listen to ideas. Some he takes a look at and others he throws out immediately. I've learned how to bring an idea to Bill. First I'll go to Paul and see what he thinks. Then the idea will work its way up to Bill. He won't hesitate to use an idea if he thinks it will enhance the offense. It's funny: I get satisfaction when one of my ideas is approved, sometimes more satisfaction than from throwing a touchdown pass. Being able to call plays for Bill Walsh is an achievement in itself. There are times when I try to guess with him, try to figure out what he's going to do, and I'm completely wrong. All week long I bitch and moan to Paul that a certain play Bill put into the system that week isn't going to work.

"God, Paul, I hate this play, there's no way this play is going anywhere," I'll complain. Then Sunday comes rolling around and the play I hated scores a touchdown. Maybe that's why people call him a genius. I've gotten a lot off my chest writing about Bill, trying to understand him. Both of us have come a long way and finally have gained mutual respect. You've got to understand that we're involved in a big business. There are so many things at stake that it tends to do strange things to a person's head.

You know all about that. No matter what kind of business you're involved in—from the janitor to the actor—the pressure is always there. It's a fact of life and all of us have to deal with it in our own way. This is something I've come to realize. Bill has to cope with different pressures than I do. It's as simple as that. I think I'm learning to deal with the situation, and I only hope he can too.

My relationship with Bill is mercurial but at the same time ironic. We both worked hard to get where we are and we both live for Sunday. I live to get out on the field, while he lives to pace the sidelines and play the role of master strategist, matching wits with the man across the field from him. I admire him for this. At this point in his life, he's not going to make many changes in his football career. You know what they say—you can't teach an old dog new tricks. Maybe he will tire of the game and move on to a new endeavor. If that happened I would miss Bill Walsh. I know we'll never be close friends, but in reality not too many people get close to their boss. Despite our differences, I've learned a lot about the game and maybe a little bit about life from the fellow with the white hair. One thing's for certain—he's an individualist, a person I'll never forget.

Playing Quarterback

He called me Joe Banana.

If you knew Chuck Abramski, my high school coach, you would say I got off lucky being tagged with that nickname. Coach Abramski was an intense little guy with a smile and a cigar in his mouth. Under his guidance, and that of our quarterback coach, Jeff Petrucci, I learned to throw the football on the run.

Looking back, I realize their teaching was important. They shaped my playing style. Ringgold High's offense had me throwing on the move, and it became second nature to me. When people talk about my style, they mention my ability to find a receiver and hit him when I'm on the run. Well, it all started in high school.

This is where I started to feel the color. Feeling the color is how I'm able to tell when I'm getting pressured in the pocket. When I come out of the huddle to take the snap from center, my eyes are focused straight ahead on the defense. I'm looking to see if the "D" is in a strange formation. At the same time I'm making sure my teammates are lined up correctly. Then I look at the defensive front. Many times they're lined up in a 34 (three linemen, four linebackers) and I call out the defensive front. Then I look over the defensive backfield to check their coverage. Some teams tip their hand. This is called "reading," and it's still going on when the ball is snapped. Many times a defensive back will take a step up toward our offensive line before the snap from center. This could mean a big play for the 49ers.

As the ball is snapped I picture the play. It's like a movie running through my mind. If the defense is showing blitz, I'm looking for our "hot" receiver. That's the receiver who is designated to get the ball if the blitz is on. Then I quickly determine what our number-one play is for a strong-side safety blitz or weak-side safety blitz.

Sounds like a lot to think about in a short amount of time, right? But a good quarterback damn well better be able to concentrate and think fast or he's in big—as in bone-breaking—trouble.

When the defense puts on a strong rush I see the colors. I only see colors, not faces, helmets, arms, or legs. Just that wall. If the 49ers are wearing red jerseys and our opponents white, my vision picks up the color changes. If the wall of colors quickly changes from red to white in the first two steps of my dropback, things register automatically. This is especially true for color changes up the middle. I move out of the pocket fast when that happens. A lot of people, including Bill and my teammates, criticize me for bailing out in a hurry. Defenders rushing up the middle are on me so fast they can inflict pain in my rib area. If I was looking at an individual's face, my reaction time would be slow. My method works.

Remember, what I've described takes place in about three seconds. It happens faster than it took you to read about it. This reaction is instinct combined with years and years of practice.

Besides the pure football stuff I learned from coach Abramski, he also taught me that you can't judge a book by its cover. He screamed, cursed, and badgered his players but he always cared about us and our future. He was a boisterous, outgoing guy. In fact, a lot of the parents didn't like his style.

On several occasions he smacked a guy on the helmet. I mean a hit, not a love tap. And was he ever explosive.

One afternoon the team was watching films of Abramski during a game. He was smoking a cigar and something that happened on the field really got him mad. Chuck threw the cigar down, tried to kick it, and fell on his ass. We all cracked up and even the coach had to laugh.

Abramski might have been a screaming skull—"Mr. Intensity"—but he didn't take himself seriously. Let's face it, some coaches are jerks and phonies. Some of the screamers just yell to cover up their weaknesses. Others, who come across as good guys or real mellow, are SOBs. Abramski had his priorities straight. His number-one concern was his kids. If one of his players—any player, not just a starter or star—came to him and said he wanted to get into college, Coach would stay on the phone for days until he placed the boy in a college. He would pull every string he had to help someone get into school.

When he first arrived on the scene at Ringgold, he told the principal and the parents that he wasn't doing any coaching until his team got new equipment. He fussed until he got his way. Again, he was thinking about his players. I was lucky to play for him. He cared about me and helped me become a fundamentally sound player.

I also developed some other tendencies in high school, such as my dislike for practice. The further you advance as a player, the more involved practice and preparation becomes. With the 49ers my day starts at 8:30 A.M. with quarterback meetings. For about four hours. I watch films of the opponent's defense, followed by forty-five minutes for lunch. Practice usually starts at about 1:30 P.M. It runs until 3:30, and then there's another meeting that lasts until 5:00.

What do you think a meeting with quarterbacks and receivers is like? All businesslike, top-secret skull sessions, where we sit in a hushed, dark room, watching film and listening to our quarterback coach Paul Hackett lay down the law? No way.

Our meeting room is in total disorder. It's like those experimental, or open, classrooms that educators were bringing to public schools in the early 1970s. I guess you could call our meeting room an insult laboratory. Anybody who really believes pro football strategy is akin to brain surgery is fooling him or herself. When I read that some hotshot network producer says pro football is a "complicated" game and his network telecast is making a complicated game more understandable, I want to suggest this gent attend one of our meetings. He would find out they're a place where the best insults are traded. If a player is coming to the 49ers and he doesn't have thick skin, he better borrow some rawhide before he enters the meeting.

Paul goes over plays and discusses pass routes. The kidding and insults start when we're going over plays and someone makes a mistake on film. Not only will Paul play back our mistakes over and over again, everyone in the room will tell you how stupid you looked on such and such a play. We all take part in sticking the needle in. Rookies take awhile to get into it, and the quiet players, like Skeets Nehemiah, shy away. We've developed a language all our own, codes that only people in that room understand. For example, when a receiver is caught loafing—not finishing a route—we refer to it as cruising. When someone is cruising on film we whistle the theme from the TV show *Love Boat.*

Everyone takes the kidding pretty well. There are some who we watch out for because their moods change abruptly. I try to read Freddie Solomon carefully. During our 1985 training camp, I was concerned that Bill might cut Freddie because he had drafted Jerry Rice, the fellow known as "World" at Mississippi Valley State, his alma mater. Jerry might be a burner but if I was a betting man I would put my two cents on Freddie in a foot race against any starting wide receiver in the NFL.

Freddie doesn't take criticism well when he's in one of his all-business moods. He's dedicated to the game. He needs complete concentration when he's improving a move or correcting a mistake. Freddie could be the moodiest person on the team but his reason is valid: He's a perfectionist who wants to get his game down.

I can remember one day during the '84 season when we were running a post pattern to Freddie in practice. I hit him right in the hands and he dropped the ball. Under normal circumstances, that would be it. Freddie would have returned to the line and waited for his turn to run the pattern again. But I told Freddie to run it again. Freddie dropped the ball again and his mates showed no mercy. They gave him a lot of lip and he responded by kicking the ball as hard as he could.

During our second run at the Super Bowl in '84, Freddie got mad during halftime in one game and stomped a stool. Wood just scattered all over the locker room. Everyone kept their mouths shut, but the next week, during practice, we all came on the field wearing "Stool Buster" T-shirts in honor of Casper.

It's important for me to read moods of my teammates, especially the receivers. If a person needs extra attention or help in getting something down, it's my job to recognize that fact and do something about it. Conversely, I also have to know when to leave a receiver alone. I don't want to give someone encouragement who doesn't need it. As for me, don't get the idea that I don't have my days. I can be pretty moody at times. I have a good relationship with Paul Hackett, but I can blow up. I remember one day during the '84 season when I showed up late for a meeting. It was a day when I woke up on the wrong side of the bed.

"Joe, what's the matter? You know we needed you here on time," Paul said. "There are things we need to go over that we needed you here for."

"Well, Paul, that's just the way it goes sometimes," I said in a real sarcastic tone.

He didn't say anything but when I got my next paycheck it was short a few dollars. He had fined me. And he was right; I had acted like a jerk.

I've also been known to blow up on the field when I thought a wrong play was called.

"Joe, what were you doing out there?" Paul says over the phone. I have nothing to say so I just hang up on him. Believe me, I don't feel good about doing that, but it relieves the tension. Our meetings might be loose but Paul won't tolerate certain things. He knows exactly when to pull in the reins.

There was another time during practice when I acted pretty strange. We have running and passing drills. Of course, I would rather take part in the passing drills because they're challenging. Matt and I kid about who is going to get stuck doing the running drill. In that drill, you stand there handing the ball to the running backs. Anyway, during this particular practice I wasn't throwing the ball well and Paul told me to join the running drill.

"Goddamn it," I screamed at Paul. "I always have to go down there." He gave me a strange look. He didn't know if I was kidding or not. As the words left my mouth I felt stupid, and I came back and apologized to Paul. Doesn't practice sound like fun?

Frankly, it's drudgery all the way. I don't think that many players around the league like practice. In fact, you would be hard pressed to find ten players in the NFL who like to practice.

When I go home, my day still isn't over. I eat dinner and study for two hours. By the time I'm finished I'm usually too tired to go out and do anything like taking in a movie. The only days I usually leave the house during the evening are Sunday, following a game, and Monday night, the night before our day off.

It's not as hard to memorize Bill's system as it was when I first came up. If it's a week where we don't have many new plays added to the offense, I can get away from my studies early and do other things. Jen and I like to go to the movies or out to dinner. Getting away from the routine during the week helps me relax.

Learning Bill's system is a major accomplishment. There's been a lot said about our number of offensive plays. It's hard to say exactly how many plays we'll use in a game, but there are 75 to 80 passing plays that are the basis of the system. Then we have many variations on each of those plays. When I go into a game I have about 110 plays to work with: 75 passes and 35 running plays. Initially, when I was learning the system, I would still be memorizing and picking up things on Saturday and sometimes on Sunday. Bill wouldn't hesitate to add a few new plays on game day.

The system comes automatically to me now. We receive our basic passing and running plays early in the week. When I'm given new plays, Bill and Paul expect me to have them down the next day. The hardest part isn't learning the basic plays but picking up the three or four formations we use with each. I have to remember each variation Bill wants to use in certain situations. Sometimes I'm not told which formation the coaches want. Bill will just call the play. Then it's my responsibility to set the formation. It's become second nature to me. There have been times when the coaches would give Matt and me sixty to seventy plays in the morning and we'd have them down by the afternoon. So much of our strategy is based on being precise and playing within the system.

When we come out to start a game our first twenty-five plays are scripted. In other words, we know exactly which plays we'll use to open the game. Bill has received notoriety for this technique. When we first started using a script it was limited to fifteen plays. When Bill saw it would work, he kept increasing the number.

The first twenty-five plays are ones he believes will get us into the end zone from a normal down-and-distance progression. The sequence isn't used if we're in an unusual situation. For instance, if we're starting a drive at our own 1-yard line or we get the ball deep in an opponent's territory, the script is dumped.

Bill went to scripting to give the people handling the ball early in the game something to anticipate. It gave them an added edge. We didn't work our way down the field worrying about what plays were going to be called. It refreshes my mind going into a game because I can review everything that might happen in the early minutes. Bill won't hesitate to dump the script if he doesn't feel comfortable with our field position. We may want to go left because of a particular blocking scheme we want to use. If the script prohibits us from doing that, Bill will put it away and go back to it later, during another part of the game.

Bill is unpredictable. Sometimes I'll be able to guess what he is going to call, but not very often. When I'm on the field I have my own ideas of what he might like to do, but he has so many plays and so many variations of each play that it really makes it hard to second-guess him. Anyway, I don't get paid for guessing what he's going to do next. What the 49ers pay me for is executing and winning. Although we get paid whether we win or lose, we all have an obligation to the organization and our teammates. Of course, we also are playing for the fans.

I think they're great. I don't know how anyone else feels, but without the fans I would be next to nothing. There's no doubt in my mind that I wouldn't have reached my playing level without the people—people who come from all walks of life to watch the San Francisco 49ers play football.

They are part of a crazy phenomenen in American sports and society. I'm lucky to be involved in a love affair with our fans. Even when I disappoint them, I know they'll be back. I know they will forgive me. It's a special relationship for me. They give me strength and courage.

While the fans are an inspiration, I'm not going to be a phony and say they are the main reason I'm playing the game. Deep inside of me, I've always been playing for myself, my family, and my teammates. I play hard, I play in pain because I want to pour it out for the team. I love them. When you've been playing the game all your life you realize the ultimate compliment comes from your teammates, the fellows with whom you not only play but also share both the good and bad times.

It's personally satisfying knowing that I'm out there doing the best I can. When the game is over I just want to look at myself in the mirror—win or lose—and know I gave it everything I had, that I didn't let anyone down. That's my number-one priority. I want to know that I played the game straight from the heart. I'm lucky to be on a veteran team that has enjoyed some major accomplishments. I remember one evening during training camp in 1985 when some of us went out for dinner. We talked about the things we had accomplished since we'd been together. Our success meant so much more because the same people shared the wins and losses. If a number of players had played for San Francisco only briefly it wouldn't have been the same. A lot of teams in the league have that revolving-door syndrome, and it takes something away from the close feeling.

For me, it's been like growing up with a family. A kid who moves from house to house doesn't ever experience that neighborhood feeling. Memories are faces on the run. Relating to the same people day after day, year after year, is special. The fellows on the 49ers are special. They're the brothers I never had.

If one of us is having family-related or money-related problems, someone on the team is there to talk it out. I'm not saying it's Utopia. When we're losing and things are going bad, no one wants to hear about someone's personal problems. It's best to have troubles during a winning season.

There's also a certain amount of jealousy. But when it gets down to the nitty-gritty, we stick together on the field and leave our jealousies in the locker room. I know some of my teammates are jealous of me. After a game one time I was talking on the telephone in the locker room. At least I *had* been talking. I had the telephone up to my ear but it had gone dead. Another player, who was around the corner from me, was complaining fairly loudly to another player.

"The only reason Montana is getting big bucks is because Eddie and him are tight," he said, referring to Mr. DeBartolo, the owner of the 49ers.

I'd be the first to admit that I have a good relationship with Mr. DeBartolo. He's a Notre Dame graduate. He's also from an Italian family, and that has led to a special friendship. But it hurt me that a teammate would minimize my contributions to the team. There's always going to be criticism, but there's also going to be some glory to go along with the bad times. Either way, as long as I go out on the field and know I tried my best I feel OK.

I've learned a lot about playing quarterback and a lot about dealing with people, thanks to the 49ers. What makes someone really good at the position is if he can combine a cautious attitude with the ability to recognize and read a defense quickly. Forget about all the nonsense about quarterbacks who, as broadcasters say, can throw the ball 70 years downfield. When I say "cautious," I don't mean that you worry about every pass you throw or tiptoe around back there. For a quarterback the game is at least 70 percent mental, and I can't afford to worry about every little thing. My job is to keep the offense flowing, keep that ball alive, and avoid the big mistake. The quarterbacks who avoid the big mistake are winners—it's as simple as that. If you don't put too much pressure on your defense you will win the game.

A quarterback has to be half psychiatrist and a little bit crazy. Certainly anyone who is set up to have his ribs broken can't always be playing with a full deck. I have to laugh when some QBs put on the macho act. Anyone who knows anything about the game knows that a quarterback is putting his body on the line every time he takes the snap from center. One thing is for certain: With my slight build I've been lucky to remain relatively injury free during my career. In your program I'm listed at six feet, two inches, 190 pounds. Actually, my weight fluctuates between 190 and 195. One day during our '85 training camp I was in the cafeteria eating one of my "big" lunches: a bowl of chicken chow mein with rice, a cheese sandwich, and some potato chips. I had a "heavy" dessert—yogurt.

"Hey, Joe, you look a little on the skinny side," one of the coaches said. "How much do you weigh?"

"About one-ninety, Coach," I said.

He would have had a fit if he knew my true weight, which was barely 185 pounds. The coaches want me to maintain my top weight so I'm stronger throughout the entire season. They know my weight fluctuates and it bothers them.

Most of my life, I've been a notorious junk-food addict. McDonald's, BK (as in Burger King), Wendy's, and Taco Bell were my hangouts until Jen made me realize that I was poisoning myself. But the stuff was so tasty I couldn't resist it. Give me a cheeseburger and I was in paradise. I finally realized that constantly eating this fast food wasn't doing me any good, and now I'm committed to keeping my body fat low. Because I "occasionally" overthrow a receiver, my teammates sometimes call me "Weight Room."

Once in a while I actually inflict physical punishment on some unsuspecting soul. My "magic" moment came during a game with the St. Louis Cardinals. Big E. J. Junior, the Birds' fine linebacker, intercepted one of my passes cleanly and was taking it back for an easy touchdown. All E.J. wanted to do was run into the end zone via a route that went through me. He wanted to drill me between the 1 and 6 on my uniform.

Now this was serious business. E.J. smelled a touchdown. The man was an irritated Brahman bull on the loose. The way I was taught to tackle in high school was to get as low as I could and go for the ankles. A sensible man would have simply played dead, just become a hunk of liquid Silly Putty.

Not me. I figured I would take a shot at slowing down this big dude. I closed my eyes and hoped for the best. I knew I'd managed to get down real low. In fact, my body was so low that my helmet hit E.J.'s shins. When I opened my eyes and picked myself off the ground I couldn't believe what had happened. The monster, E. J. Junior, was actually hurt and stretched out on the field. I couldn't believe I wasn't the one who was knocked silly and waiting for the stretcher. But after I pinched myself I realized I had pulled off the ultimate quarterback's fantasy. Of all the places on E.J.'s body, I'd gotten lucky and found the most vulnerable, the tenderest.

I got a lot of mileage out of that "hit." It was like a pitcher hitting a home run. I was strutting my stuff. "Hey, defense," I joked. "I'm bad, super bad, I hurt him. He doesn't want any part of me," I said, doing my best Richard Pryor imitation.

Just kidding, Mr. Junior, sir.

When a quarterback is dealing in reality he knows his offensive line is the key to his success. The men on the 49ers offensive line are the key to not only my but our team's success. It's been a pleasure to watch them develop for seven years. You don't hear much about offensive line play. Not many fans realize how hard an offensive lineman's job is. They must have both mental and physical coordination or we won't win. As I explained earlier, their moves are synchronized, just like figure skaters. They play against the greatest athletes in the game, 289- to 300-pound linemen who run like halfbacks and jump like NBA power forwards.

The youngest member of our line is our left tackle, William "Bubba" Paris. Bubba is listed at six feet six, 295 pounds. But he is probably six feet six, 310. Bubba was getting fined every time his weight went over 300 pounds. He found a way to fool the coaches. For about three weeks he was weighing in at 295, fooling them by leaning on a juice machine next to the scale.

I'm always amazed when he rides his little bicycle around training camp. The tires look like they are flat but Bubba keeps on pedaling. Even though people kid him about his weight, when he plays he really gets the job done. He's usually blocking the guy who's rushing on the blind side of the quarterback. That's where the defense puts its best pass rusher the majority of the time. A defensive lineman who can get in and rush from an angle where I can't see him can end my career. Even during his rookie season, Bubba showed that he was destined to be a good one.

He also had some help from one of the best, our left guard John Ayers, who plays next to him. At six feet five, 265 pounds, John, who played his college ball at West Texas State, is the most underrated offensive lineman in the NFL. Frankly, he doesn't get much attention or recognition because the media tends to focus on one of his line partners, our right guard Randy Cross. But think about this: How many offensive linemen can handle Lawrence Taylor, the great New York Giants linebacker? Not many. Has L.T. been a factor in the games we've played against the Giants? No.

John works harder than anyone I know in football. I'm waiting for the day he gets the recognition he deserves. However, there's one thing I can do without. His favorite practical joke is spitting a glob of tobacco on my shoes. Well, I guess you can't ask for everything in a lineman.

Moving over to Randy Cross, what he's done speaks for itself. The average football fan can name only a few offensive linemen in the NFL. Randy is in this category, and I'm not talking about just 49er fans. He's not only a physical force but he's one of the team's leaders. Randy's style of line play fits our offense perfectly. He's big, strong, and mobile, which is just what's needed when he has to pull or execute some deception-type blocks.

Next to Randy is tackle Keith Fahnhorst. I couldn't believe it took people so long to realize that he was a Pro Bowl–caliber player. I watch a lot of film, and I know there are few people playing who are better than Keith. He is another man who faces off against superstars. Just ask Jack Youngblood. Keith went up against Jack twice a year before Jack retired from the Los Angeles Rams, and Keith did a good job against him. He has also had tremendous days against Joe Klecko of the New York Jets and my buddy Too Tall Jones.

And then there's the hub of the line, the gentleman whom I'm "close to," center Fred Quillan. Fred is somewhat of a joker. When we met again at the opening of the '85 training camp, his first words to me were "Joe, I really missed your hands." People always tease Fred, telling him he wouldn't be anything without the guys on either side of him, Cross and Ayers. Of course he can do more, as a blocker, than most centers in the league. As you can see, there are so many elements and individuals that help make a good quarterback that no one person can do it alone. I've been lucky to play with some great people who understand and support what I'm trying to do. I can't ask for anything more than that.

Jennifer and Alexandra

It was a nervous time for me as I flew into Los Angeles International Airport—or, as the baggage tag reads, "LAX"—to do a commercial for Schick razors in February 1984. Larry Muno was meeting me to drive me to a studio where I was going to be fitted for my costume. I had done commercials before, but this was the first time I would be working with another person.

My first taste of Madison Avenue had been after we won the Super Bowl in 1982 and advertising agencies took an interest in me. Even though I liked the idea of acting, I was hesitant. My body needed a rest. But what the heck. You've got to grab it while you're hot, and I've always been interested in learning something new. So I was to go on camera for Concorde watches. I flew the red-eye from Los Angeles to New York with Larry.

I had gotten one hour of sleep when I arrived in New York. I took a quick shower. As soon as I jumped out of the shower—at 6 A.M.—I knew it was going to be a day where I would be running on fumes: pure adrenaline.

It also happened to be the first day of the NFL Players Association strike. There was a lot on my mind, but I tried to put football aside for a day so I could give a good performance in the commercial. The job sounded easy enough. I would say a few lines, meet some people, and that would be it.

Was I ever wrong.

The advertising agency hired an arm model to wear the watch when they moved in for a close-up of it. All I was supposed to do was catch a pass and say something like "The only time I can't wear it is during a game; they won't let me."

The director, the guy who was running the show, wanted everything perfect, but that was not to be: His arm model never showed up and I had to fill in. I had to hold my arm perfectly straight so it would just pass through the lens. This would make it appear that my arm was in motion. They needed to illuminate the watch, and I was surrounded by huge hot lights. If I moved my hand closer or farther away from the camera the watch went out of focus. If I twisted my wrist either way it would cause a glare on the face of the watch. Now I can understand why hand models get paid so much. They must have nerves of steel. The more I thought about keeping my arm perfectly still, the more I moved it one way or another. Believe me, it wasn't an easy task. Don't get the feeling that I was an ingrate, but I was exhausted from flying across the country and having to go right to work. I didn't understand why they couldn't have shot the commercial in San Francisco. I was also nervous because the strike was in its first day and I knew I wanted to work out the next day. I had no idea how long the walkout would last.

When we finished the TV commercial, they sent me to another studio in midtown Manhattan to get my picture taken for the print advertisement. By this time both Larry and I were getting mad. We tried to get the agency to postpone the session with the photographer. It was 6 P.M. and I was falling asleep. Although I was getting paid $30,000 for one day's work, I felt I was being used.

Finally I finished the pictures, and I headed for LaGuardia

Airport at 8 P.M. for another all-night flight. But that's show business.

There was a more professional feeling in the Schick commercial. The agency was serious. It was a bigger production than the Concorde spot. I was going to be a cowboy and work with Jennifer Wallace, a model who had appeared as the "Schick Sheriff." Believe me, I was scared. I had the same feelings I had had when I walked into the Kingdome for that exhibition game my rookie year. I would rather have been facing a full blitz from the Raiders. At least I would have known what to expect.

"I can't do this, it's making me nervous. I've never worked with anyone else," I told Larry.

"Hey, Joe, come on, you're overreacting. It's going to work out. You're just nervous because it's something new. You never know what this might lead to," Larry said.

As it turned out he was certainly intuitive.

All my nervousness disappeared when I met Jennifer. I was trying on my cowboy duds when she walked into the room. Now, people always say that certain folks light up a room. Most of the time, though, that's an overstatement. It's a romantic cliché, but I honestly had never seen anyone do it.

That day, I saw the real thing. I remember how tall and striking Jennifer looked. Not only is she tall—five feet eleven—she is really tan. Jen spends a lot of time outdoors and takes good care of herself.

The other thing I remember is how she treated people. When she talked to anybody, from the director to the person who got the coffee, she asked a lot of questions. She's truly interested in people. This is a quality I don't see often. She makes people feel so comfortable and important. That's a wonderful characteristic and not many people have it.

Jen broke the ice with me quickly.

"Finally they got someone who doesn't have to stand on an apple crate," Jen said to the director. She started laughing and I cracked up. She'd loosened things up right away.

Her personality was infectious. All I wanted was to get a chance to sit down and talk with her, to get a chance to know her. But we had a job to do. We were waiting to move on to the next step and the people from the advertising agency kept us busy by taking pictures as we chatted on the set. After the photos were taken, Jen had to leave. I was disappointed. She was like a magnet for me. This was unusual. I'm on the quiet side, but there was something about her that was drawing me out of my shell.

The following day we went to work in earnest. As I'd found out during my first experience, doing commercials is tough and time-consuming. There isn't any opportunity for small talk—it's all business. I tried to find out what her dinner plans were. I kept hanging around the set to get up enough courage to ask her to dinner.

The following night we went out to dinner with the people from Schick, and I drove Jennifer home. "Jennifer, do you think we could get together for dinner? I really want to see you again. I want to talk to you, I want to get to know you."

"Joe," she said, "that's fine. But I've got to be honest with you. I don't want to get serious with you or anyone. My career comes first. I'm not ready to get into a relationship."

My heart dropped somewhere south of my knees.

"That's OK, Jennifer. I'm not ready for a serious relationship either."

When we finished doing the commercial, I still wanted to see her even though she'd put it on the line. Fortunately, I did a lot of traveling between San Francisco and Los Angeles to take care of business with Larry, and this gave me a chance to see Jen. It was really great. We ran on the beach and threw a football around. I never experienced this kind of relationship with a woman. She was a friend. We seemed to have a lot in common and we communicated so well. I felt relaxed and happy. There was no pressure.

This was something unusual for me. My other relationships with women had been pressure-filled. I always watched what I said, I never felt relaxed. Maybe I was still in the process of maturing. With Jen things came naturally; nothing was forced, everything was spontaneous.

Before I met Jen I was lonely. I had a hard time living by myself. When I was faced with doing things for myself, I realized some of the domestic things I had taken for granted were actually hard. I never had to deal with them before. At the same time, being alone was something of a relief because I didn't have to worry about what I did or said. I could relax and do as I pleased.

Jen and I kept our relationship going through the entire summer. When I was in L.A. I stayed at a hotel and visited her as much as I could. We would talk, laugh, and work out together. She convinced me to take better care of myself. As I said, I was a notorious junk-food freak. Jennifer watches what she eats and she taught me to treat my body with respect. If I took care of myself it would have a positive effect on my on-the-field performance. For the first time in my life I was feeling physically strong—"Muscles" Montana. My state of mind was also improving.

Despite this fantastic relationship, I didn't want to get married again. Maybe I was scared that if I married Jennifer it would change the special relationship we had. Who knows? All I was certain of was that I was happy and didn't want to lose the feeling.

Toward the end of the summer of 1984 my feelings began to deepen. My relationships never had this kind of meaning, this kind of sharing. She was something different—a friend and a lover.

I sensed Jen was having the same feelings, but I was reluctant to ask her how she felt about us. I didn't want to spoil what we had. If this was as far as our relationship was going to go I just wanted to hang on to it. Maybe I was reading too much into the situation, but Jen was saying things that made me believe she felt the same way I did.

Finally, I said the hell with it. I was going to take a chance and ask her to marry me right after a preseason game in August in San Francisco. Now, I wasn't going to sit her down and ask her to marry me. I wanted to make it special, something Jen would remember. I know a fellow who flies a plane and displays all kinds of advertising banners from the tail: everything from EAT AT KATHY'S to HAPPY HOUR, ALL YOU CAN DRINK.

My plan was to rent his plane and have him pull a banner asking Jen to marry me. Business was good for my pal. He didn't know if he could handle my request because he was really busy. Finally he got a cancellation and said he would carry the banner. It would simply read JEN WILL YOU MARRY ME? JOE.

It was a beautiful Saturday afternoon. I asked Jen if she wanted to go to our favorite park in San Francisco and meet some of our friends. She is an inquisitive lady. She wondered why I wanted to go to the park after a game. Obviously she was wondering what I was up to.

I knew approximately what time the plane was going to buzz over us, and Jen and I arrived at the park in plenty of time to catch it. This would really turn out to be a day to remember. My mission was to maneuver her into a position where she could see the plane. We walked around the park over and over again as I was trying to cast occasional glances at the sky to see if it was coming. Let's face it: For me to expect I could walk around the park with my head swiveling around in the air without Jen noticing that something was up was next to impossible. We kept walking and finally sat down on a bench. I was sweating it out because my buddy was late. I kept wondering if he was going to show at all.

"Joe, what are we doing?" Jen asked. She was getting very suspicious and I was coming up with bogus excuses. I wasn't having any luck.

Finally I saw the plane, but it was flying right over us and we couldn't see the banner. "Look at that plane," I said. "It looks like Russ Francis. He's got a biplane. Let's take a closer look." At least that gave me an excuse to keep walking so we could get in a position where Jen could see the banner.

Finally she saw the banner, but we were standing directly under the plane so she couldn't read it. I moved her to the right and at last she got a good look. Our position didn't matter. I wanted to give Jen my heart and she knew it. She said yes and I just can't express the feeling that came over me. It was like a long search had finally ended.

For the first time I had made the decision to ASK someone to marry me. And I'm so lucky. I can't explain the feeling I've carried inside of me since we agreed to spend our lives together. Six months later we were married.

I've learned a lot from Jen. She's helped me to open up to people, something I've had a hard time doing. If I shy away from a situation, she understands and helps me in her own way.

I don't know about other sports, but football demands a lot of time, and it makes family life very difficult. It takes an extraordinary woman to cope with it. Some want to be a part of every moment. That's hard to handle. A player has to play the game with no interference. He needs a person to understand his moods but he also needs someone to be there, sharing the good and bad times. This sounds selfish but it's just a fact of football life. If your mate is always sticking her two cents in, telling you what to do when it comes to handling the pressure of being a quarterback, things are going to be difficult.

Baseball players can take their families to training camp, but we can't. When Jen was pregnant with Alexandra she was alone. Not only was she alone, but she had to find us a place to live in San Francisco. She never said anything about it. She did come up to camp to spend a little time with me in 1985.

She has a career of her own as a mother and a model, but she's always there to help me. During the 1985 Super Bowl against the Miami Dolphins, Jen took care of all the arrangements for my family. That was a crazy time for her. It was the first time she went through Super Bowl madness. Instinctively, Jen knew to leave me alone when I was feeling the pressure. She knew how to excuse us tactfully when my family—whom I love dearly—wanted to chit-chat the night before the game.

She has changed my feelings about football too. After a loss I'll be going over all the things I did wrong: why I didn't hit this receiver or what I should have done in a certain situation. Finally Jennifer will say, "Let's go home and see the Pumpkin" (our nickname for Alexandra). "Joe, she doesn't know or care what happened out there today."

Alexandra has put life in perspective for Jen and me. Both of us are career-oriented people; our lives revolve around our professions. I don't think there's anything wrong with that, but when you get right down to it, all the money in the world can't buy a happy family life. I have something that's more important than football. It's not that I don't still love the game, but now I'm secure in knowing I really can give love to my family. I can have another life, something very important to me. It's made me a stronger person. I hope it has also made me a better person.

I always wanted to be a father, but when I first found out that Jen was pregnant, I was scared. I was afraid that I wouldn't be a good father. How would I raise my child? What would I do? I knew nothing about being a parent. Sure, I knew what Mom and Dad had done, but I believed they were so special that there was no way I could duplicate what they did for me. One thing I was sure of: I didn't want to make any mistakes. Putting it simply, I was baffled; I didn't know where to begin. Where does a quarterback/father start? I tried to learn about children during Jen's pregnancy, and I went to Lamaze class with her every chance I got. Actually, we were lucky. Elaine, our teacher, would come to our home for the lessons.

In October of the '85 season, the 49ers came back to San Francisco from a game against the Atlanta Falcons. When I got home that Sunday night Jen began feeling contractions. They were irregular and weak and it was late at night, so we didn't do anything about them.

The next day we were going to look at some property in Redwood City where we plan to build a house in 1986. Later that day we were supposed to go to Lamaze class. Elaine had been so nice that we wanted to go to her house in San Jose to meet her family. But while we were in Redwood City looking at the property, Jen began feeling uncomfortable.

She was in no shape to drive to San Jose. We went straight home and the contractions continued through the night. They were irregular and varied in intensity. We didn't know if this was the real thing, but since some of the contractions were so long and hard, Jen thought she should pay a visit to her doctor the next morning.

We arrived at the doctor's office at 11 A.M. that Tuesday. The doctor examined Jen and found her cervix had dilated. Because her contractions were so erratic, he hooked her to an IV and put a drug in it that would control them. It was time to have the baby.

I was fine when I was watching the birth process but what really upset me was looking at Jen's face and seeing all the pain in it. She was pushing so hard, trying her best. I had never seen her in that kind of agony. No matter how hard she pushed, the baby just wouldn't come out.

The pain was excruciating. It had to be worse than being blind-sided in the spine by Too Tall. Jen was suffering and began to cry. I was standing in front of her; she needed someone to hold. She grabbed my ear and nearly ripped it off.

I couldn't take it. Nothing I'd ever experienced on a football field equaled this. I nearly passed out and had to sit down. Jen was hooked to a monitor and so I could tell just when the pain was coming. Instead of her contractions zigzagging and reaching a peak, they were hard and cutting like a knife. I felt completely helpless: There was nothing I could do. After two hours the baby finally arrived. I grabbed the little girl and hugged her arms and legs.

My eyes just bubbled up in tears. It was such a relief knowing Jen and our little girl were all right.

"It's a girl," I said.

"Let me see her." I lay the baby on her chest and cut the umbilical cord. It felt so good holding the baby and seeing the relief and happiness on Jennifer's face. While going through the birth, she had kept screaming that she didn't know how anyone could go through this agony more than once.

After she saw Alexandra, the first words out of her mouth were "I want to have another child."

As I said, the Pumpkin has put life in perspective for me.

During the 1985 season I had my share of bad games. Sometimes when we were returning home on the plane a teammate would remind me that Alexandra was waiting for me. Now I have another world to go to. When I'm finished with a game and see the Pumpkin, football doesn't exist, I forget about the game. I see things differently. I just want to come out of the game healthy so I can see my baby. When we lose I'll go into her room and ask her when she is going to talk to me. I'll ask her to say "Mommy" or "Daddy." I call her the Pumpkin or Egg Head because she doesn't have much hair yet.

Even though I know she doesn't understand me, I make her laugh. Once I told Egg Head I was going to dye her head a bright shade of purple for Easter.

I think Alexandra has changed Jennifer's goals. She wants to go back to work but it won't necessarily be acting or modeling. Jen's got her eye on a baby boutique in San Francisco or L.A.

Sometimes I think about what's going to happen when my career is over. I'd like to establish something for Jennifer and me, something we can do together and enjoy. Life is complete for me; I feel so fulfilled.

Now I know there is definitely life after football.

14

Another Super Bowl: Montana Meets Marino

Some folks might have considered us lucky to make it to the National Football Conference Championship game in January 1984. Our record was 10-6. We had had a rough season and squeaked into the championship game by beating the Detroit Lions 24–23.

In the Detroit game we got a lucky break. Eddie Murray, the Lions' field-goal kicker, missed a last-second chip shot that would have won the game for them. The soggy turf at Candlestick Park had a lot to do with his missing the field goal. Although the turf had been replaced in 1982, it never took hold. Eddie wasn't used to kicking in the Candlestick muck and mire. I believe he just lost his concentration. Moe was used to kicking on our home field but the real secret to Moe's success is his ability to concentrate under any circumstances. That is what makes a consistent field-goal kicker.

So we squeaked by the Lions and had to move on to another liquid turf—the Robert F. Kennedy Memorial Stadium—and a date with the Washington Redskins, featuring the irrepressible John Riggins and my fellow Notre Dame alumnus Joe Theismann. Although the Skins came into the game with a better record than the 49ers, we weren't exactly pushovers. We had scored 541 points during the regular season. Ironically, the only team to beat us out in the most-points-scored category was Washington.

We didn't play well during the first half. It wasn't that we were relaxing or uptight. It was simply a matter of missing on a couple of long passes down the field that would have put us ahead of the Skins. They built a 21–0 lead late in the third quarter. This was the point in the game where the referees' calls started affecting us. The first incident happened when Joe Theismann tried hooking up with Art Monk. The pass was incomplete but Washington caught a big break when we were hit with a pass-interference penalty. The penalty was magnified because the previous three times the 49ers had had the ball Moe missed two field goals and Freddie fumbled in a key situation.

We gave the Redksins great field position when Freddie fumbled. The Skins were leading 7–0 at the time, and he was neck-tied by Darrell Green. Green's version of a public hanging resulted in us losing the ball at our own 36-yard line. Theismann immediately went to work, hitting Monk for a 13-yard gain. Riggins, a.k.a. "Riggo" or "The Diesel," ran to the 2-yard line. Then came the first of a series of pass-interference calls. Joe dropped back to pass and hit Monk near the left sideline. The pass was incomplete but the refs claimed that Ronnie bumped Art. The questionable call gave the Redskins an automatic first down at our 6-yard line. It took Theismann three plays before Riggins squeaked his way into the end zone from 1 yard out, giving Washington a 14–0 lead.

Naturally, there were two different theories concerning Ronnie's interference penalty. Monk claimed Ronnie continued to bump him more than the 5 yards a defender is allowed according to NFL rules. Ronnie said he was running with Art, saw the football, and suddenly was mugged by Monk. "I just knocked the ball out of his hands," Ronnie told me. "If the official was going to call interference, he should have called it on Art."

The next time we got the ball we were forced to punt. The Redskins went right to work. Joe hit Charlie Brown over the middle for a 70-yard touchdown that gave the Skins a 21–0 lead with just over a minute left in the quarter. On the play, Brown found himself matched up with our versatile linebacker Keena Turner. Brown was able to outrun Keena (who has tremendous speed), Ronnie, and Dwight Hicks in the last 46 yards of his journey to the end zone.

There are two things that can happen when a team falls behind under the worst of situations. Either you bag it or you search for something that will somehow turn the momentum in your favor. Shifting the momentum in hostile territory is next to impossible. With the Redskins' band blasting "Hail to the Redskins," and the RFK crowd sure they had the 49ers rocking and reeling, I was aware that the task ahead of us was monumental. But the 49ers had been here before. We were a team who knew what gut-check time was all about. We knew how to turn a disaster into a delightful experience.

At this point in the game, I had completed only seventeen of thirty-two passes for 142 yards. It was up to me to get it started. Things began to click. We scored three quick touchdowns. I hit Mike Wilson—filling in for Dwight Clark, who was injured—for a 5-yard score. Then I hit Freddie, who became Superman, turned up the burners about three notches to catch a 76-yard touchdown pass. Then I hit Mike again for a 12-yard score. We had dodged the bullet. With 7:18 left in the game we had turned chickenshit into chicken salad. The game was all tied up.

I was feeling a little better at this point. When the momentum starts to change in a game, especially that fast and that drastically, it's really hard for the other team to stop the tidal wave. The thrust moves from your offense to your defense. The defense knows that all they have to do is hold the other team and the offense will come back on the field and take care of the rest. The Redskins knew we had seized the momentum from them and so quickly tried to regain it from us.

They attempted a reverse play on the kickoff following Mike's touchdown. Garrett took Moe's kick and handed the ball to Monte Coleman, who ran the ball to the Redskins' 40-yard line. However, the referees called Stuart Anderson, a lineman, for holding. The call pushed the ball back to the Skins' 9-yard line. Despite the shift in momentum, I knew Joe Theismann was going to go all out. Some people say Joe talks too much, that he always has an opinion. All I know about Joe is that he finds a way to get the job done. Not only will he try, he will usually succeed.

Joe moved the Skins to our 45-yard line. Now the real controversy began. The penalties would stick in my mind throughout the off-season. Joe threw deep down the left sideline to Art Monk. The ball flew over Art's head out of bounds, but the referee threw a penalty flag and called pass interference against Eric Wright. Monk claimed that Eric had pushed him, but there was no way Art could have caught that pass. Eric said it was a bad call, and Bill Walsh gave a good description of the play. He said the pass couldn't have been caught by a "ten-foot Boston Celtic." The call moved the ball to our 15-yard line and the Redskins had a first down. After Riggo carried the ball twice to our 5-yard line, another penalty was called. Theismann looked to the right corner of the end zone and saw his tight end Rick Walker, but the pass was incomplete. Again a flag was thrown, but this time it was away from the play. The refs claimed that Ronnie Lott had held Charlie Brown at the line of scrimmage. The call gave Washington a first down at our 8-yard line. Riggins ran the ball three times but could move only to the 7-yard line.

There were forty seconds left on the clock and Redskins' field-goal kicker Mark Moseley was called on to attempt a 25-yard field goal. Twenty-five yards separated the Skins from the Super Bowl. Mark kicked the ball right through the goalposts, and I felt so helpless. There would be no comebacks this day. The Skins were on their way to the Super Bowl and the 49ers would spend the spring and summer reflecting on what could have been. Was the game stolen from us? I tend to think so.

I didn't know it at the time, but this bitter loss would actually provide the San Francisco 49ers with an incentive to begin another drive to the Super Bowl in the 1984–85 season. All I remember, walking off the field in Washington that day, were my eyes meeting Ronnie Lott's. We both felt mean and disgusted. Every picture tells a story and Ronnie's face captured the 49ers' mood. He wasn't crying but his head was down. He wouldn't look up.

This was the toughest loss we had ever experienced. God, do I hate losing. That particular day I vowed we would make it to the next Super Bowl. Not only would we make it, we would win it. Despite my confidence, I was destroyed. There was no way I could watch the Raiders-Redskins Super Bowl.

But I knew eventually I would get over it. The best thing for me to do was try to forget about the game, relax, and move on to the next case.

When we reported to training camp in July '84 I picked up certain indicators that the team meant serious business. We had something to prove. Man for man we knew we were cheated out of the NFC Championship against Washington. But thinking about something and actually going out and doing it are two different things. There was a certain kind of intensity that I spotted immediately, a no-nonsense attitude. Defensive backs were playing in practice as if it were a game. They were sticking like glue. Ordinarily, as I said before, practice is practice. But in '84, we were going to do everything in our power not to be denied.

When we won the Super Bowl in 1982 we didn't have much of a running game. During this training camp everyone saw that our big backs—Wendell Tyler and Roger "Catfish" Craig— were going to make a difference. The offensive line had more incentive to block because they had runners who could make other teams worry. As I have said, our offensive line always was super capable, but now they had something to work with. One game during the '84 season against the Cleveland Browns comes to mind. Initially I saw a mass of bodies, just like a logjam. Suddenly, the line opened a huge hole. It opened so fast, it looked like those sliding glass doors in a supermarket, opening and closing in a bat of an eyelash.

When Wendell has the ball he likes to hit the hole sideways. Roger tries to duck and turn a little bit so he can get under the defenders' shoulder pads. Wendell has been accused of being a runner who fumbles a lot. This is a result of his running style. Because he runs sideways and doesn't stick the ball close to his body, he is susceptible to the fumble. I've always thought people made too much out of this. Wendell doesn't fumble any more than the great Los Angeles Rams running back Eric Dickerson. You don't hear people getting on Eric's case. Wendell tries to jump on the count. When he breaks the huddle he begins reading the defense. He's really fast getting off the ball. He's so fast that I have to be prepared when his number is called.

Roger is different. He picks his spots once he gets his hands on the ball. He runs on instinct. Although both men joined us in 1983—Wendell in a trade with the Los Angeles Rams and Roger a second-round draft choice out of the University of Nebraska—it took time for them to be incorporated into Bill's system. They both came into their own in '84, and when they did, they gave us a new dimension we didn't have before.

Our intensity during training camp carried over into the regular season, but by no means were we cakewalking. I knew the Detroit Lions—a team that always gives the 49ers trouble—weren't the best team for our first game.

I was right. It took a 55-yard punt return by Dana McLemore, who also doubles as a defensive back, to set the stage for Moe with four seconds left in the game. The game was tied 27–27 when Moe walked on the field. Of course, he never looked at the goalpost. Like a blind man feeling for a curb, he reached out for me, tapped me on the back, set up, and calmly knocked it home, giving the 49ers a 30–27 lead. As I walked off the field I wondered how Eddie Murray felt. Moe was able to do what Ed couldn't do a year ago.

We barely escaped Detroit. Next on our agenda was revenge: a date with the Washington Redskins. If someone had bottled the adrenaline we had stored inside us since we lost that NFC title game to the Skins, we could have propelled a rocket back and forth to the moon at least ten times. We blew it all out in the first quarter, opening a 27–3 lead. When we came into the locker room at halftime we were physically and emotionally drained. All our adrenaline was gone. We knew the entire second half would be gut-check time. The Skins took advantage of the fatigue factor by scoring 28 points. We hung on and scored 10 points to win the game, 37–31. I forgot revenge. Something else entered my mind; if we could win a game like this, we had a good shot at going all the way. I was excited.

Our next stop was New Orleans. I got banged up pretty bad, hurting my ribs. The pain was so bad I had to come out of the game. Matt Cavanaugh replaced me and hit Earl Cooper with a fourth-quarter touchdown pass, giving us a 30–20 win. The 49ers were rolling with a 3-0 record.

Next, Matt made his first start in two years and came on strong. He victimized the Philadelphia Eagles on their home field, leading us to a 21–9 win.

During practice the following week, I had to prepare to come back against the Atlanta Falcons. It was strange because I knew I would be playing injured; I started thinking about parts of my equipment that I hate. Number one is my hip pads. They really squeeze me; it's like being a piece of wood or metal twisted inside a vise. They take away the freedom and flexibility I feel I need to play the game. The piece of equipment I absolutely despise is my flak jacket, a large leather contraption that's like a monster bulletproof vest. I've worn it since 1982 strictly as a safety measure. A quarterback's ribs are probably the most vulnerable part of his body. When I first started wearing the jacket I believed it would take away from my game, which is largely based on quickness. Also, it prohibited me from carrying the football as close to my body as I like. The flak jacket is bulky and makes me feel muscle-bound, but now that I've learned to adapt to it, it's just another part of playing the game.

All thoughts of equipment disappeared during the Atlanta game. We needed only 14 points, as the defense shut the Falcons down, allowing them only 5 points. We headed for New York with a 5-0 record and a Monday night game with the Giants. This was our fastest start ever. I had a long run that fooled the Giants, and Dana McLemore ran a punt back 79 yards. The Giants were hit by first-half lightning and never were in the game. Chalk up a 31–10 win for the 49ers.

October 14, 1984, the day we played the Steelers in Candlestick, still is buried somewhere in my mind. Although we went into the game undefeated, I was worried. As I said before, I idolize the Steelers; they have a special place in my heart.

We were going into the game hurting. Freddie had a pulled hamstring and wouldn't be playing. Without Casper, a big piece of our attack was gone. I also knew Keith Fahnhorst wouldn't play as soon as he went out on the field. He had been suffering lower-back spasms all week. Farnie had played in ninety-five consecutive games; his streak was now stopped with Pittsburgh. We lost the game 20–17.

It was a contest that reminded me of the Washington Championship game. With 3:21 left in the game and the 49ers leading 17–10, a controversial penalty was called by field judge Don Habel. Pittsburgh had a fourth and goal at our 6-yard line. Steeler quarterback Mark Malone threw a pass that was intended for John Stallworth. Stallworth was running a crossing pattern, just a tiny bit inside the end zone. Eric Wright stretched as far as he could and batted the ball away from John. E's play was a great one but Habel, a rookie official, pulled his yellow flag and dropped it. He believed Eric stopped Stallworth by pushing him with his left hand. My initial thought was the call could have gone either way. The penalty moved the ball to our 1. On the next play, Pittsburgh was hit with an offside penalty, pushing the ball back to the 6. Malone then hit Stallworth, who outjumped Ronnie for the score. The touchdown tied the game 17–17. The penalty ultimately cost us the game.

We had lots of time to come back and win. On our first play

I passed 15 yards to Roger Craig. Two plays later disaster struck. With 2:03 left in the game. Pittsburgh's left linebacker Bryan Hinkle came out of nowhere to grab my pass. He took it back 43 yards to the 49ers' 3-yard line. The interception was a key play. It would leave Gary Anderson, the Steelers' field-goal kicker, with a shot at a 21-yard field goal. This was well within his range. He hit the field goal, and this turned out to be the Steelers' margin of victory. Hinkle's interception was a lapse on my part, a near miss. It was one of many I experienced throughout the game. As Bill likes to say, I was out of sync all day. On the Anderson interception I was trying to hit Billy Ring, who was double-covered on the sideline. Mike Wilson was running a short delay pattern over the middle and was wide open. I thought Pittsburgh's defensive set made it advantageous for me to throw to Ring. I was wrong.

Not only was Hinkle in front of Ring, but there was another defensive back behind him. When I released the ball I wanted to take it back. Hinkle had to get up in the air to pull the pass down. It wasn't an easy interception. The pattern of near misses had begun early in the game. We missed a scoring opportunity late in the first quarter. I threw a bullet down the sideline to Mike Wilson, who was the primary receiver on the play. Pittsburgh's cornerback Dwayne Woodruff, who Mike ran right by, reached up and batted the ball away. Although I threw a slingshot, the wind played tricks with the ball; it took the zip out of the pass and it never reached Mike. Ironically, on the play, D.C. was wide open, deep down the middle of the field. I just didn't see him. Dwight was free-lancing on the play, and he surprised me. He wasn't mad about the play. "Joe, I know you weren't supposed to look there," he told me after the game.

Down the stretch I began taking care of business. We had 1:36 and no time-outs left. But we believed in ourselves. I completed six of seven passes for 54 yards on the drive. We moved from our own 26-yard line to the Pittsburgh 20. Moe was in a good position to knock it home. I knew he was feeling good. He lives for these moments. When he hit the ball I felt his confidence, but when we both looked up he'd missed. It was just one of those things. We chalked it off to the Pittsburgh jinx.

Get this: In the first quarter Moe kicked a 51-yard field goal. It was his longest shot at Candlestick. But wouldn't you know it, we were penalized. Allan Kennedy, our tight end who played on the right side of the line, lined up in the backfield. This left us with six players on the line of scrimmage. The rules state that a team needs seven players on the line. Although Moe had plenty of leg, Bill decided not to go for the 56-yard attempt following the penalty.

Now we were 6-1, and immediately some sportswriters started comparing the 49ers to the 7-0 Miami Dolphins. I guess they were looking into their crystal balls, trying to find out what a Dolphins–49ers matchup would be like. The Dolphins had blasted the Steelers 31–7 one week before we lost to Pittsburgh, but Tony Dungy, the Steelers' defensive coordinator, said we were the best offense he had seen. Tony, at that time the youngest defensive coordinator in the NFL, played for Bill in 1979. He made me feel good when he said if he were starting a team he would take me over Dan Marino. Of course, I had more experience than Danny. There was one element in the game that almost went unnoticed. Roger Craig caught six passes moving out of the backfield. This was a sign of things to come. Roger's ability to turn these short passes into big gainers eventually would be a key part of our offense. In two weeks Roger caught thirteen passes for 126 yards.

We came right back the following week, beating Houston 34–21. This was the halfway mark in the season, and I completed twenty-five of thirty-five passes for 356 yards and three touchdowns. I was feeling really good. I was feeling so good that despite the fact we had a number of players out with the flu, we went into Anaheim and beat the Rams 33–0. I knew we were on a roll.

The next game wouldn't be so easy. Cincinnati came into Candlestick with revenge on their minds. Not only was the memory of their loss to us in the Super Bowl still lingering in their minds but, Sam Wyche, Cincinnati's head coach, had something to prove. Remember, he worked for Bill as our quarterback coach between 1979 and 1982. Sam then moved to the University of Indiana for one year before becoming head coach of the Bengals. San Francisco–Cincinnati is a true rivalry, not only because of Sam's link to Bill but because of Bill's memories of his years under Paul Brown. As far as my feelings, I had a good relationship with Sam. I knew he respected me but also was aware that he had a good idea of what I was capable of doing. Did he ever! I was intercepted four times, but with 1:39 left in the game I threw a 4-yard touchdown pass, giving us a 23-17 win.

In our next game, against the Cleveland Browns, we took control from the beginning. The Browns lost the opening kickoff and we went to work. Roger Craig and I scored two touchdowns each and we went on to blow the Browns away 41-7. It was our largest margin of victory up to that point. I remember the look on Bill's face after the game. To say he was on top of the world would have been an understatement.

The next week against Tampa Bay we were hit with a disaster. Ronnie Lott separated his shoulder and we lost the heart of our defense. But "The Warrior," Fred Dean, got real nasty and led us to a 24–17 win.

The next week we clinched the NFC western-division title by beating New Orleans 35–3. We were 12-1. With three games left in the regular season, we put the blinders on. The 49ers didn't care what anyone was writing, saying, or how any other team—including the Miami Dolphins—was playing. This was time for the finishing kick.

First came the Atlanta Falcons. We had never much cared for Atlanta. At one time they were the dirtiest team in the NFL. The Falcons made the Raiders look like choirboys. Their defense enjoyed spearing people. That's when a player slams into your body, helmet first—usually in the rib area—after the referee has blown the whistle to end the play. The Falcons especially liked spearing the quarterback. It got to the point that whenever someone on the 49ers was tackled there would be a huge pileup. Bobb McKittrick told his offensive linemen to dive into the pile head first and throw bodies off whoever was holding the ball.

I experienced one of the scariest moments on a football field during a 1983 game against Atlanta. Renaldo Nehemiah was running a shallow crossing pass pattern and the Falcons fooled us. They ran a defensive back with him. They disguised their defense. The Falcons looked like they were playing straight man-to-man except on Renaldo's side of the field. The defender was playing bump-and-run with Renaldo. I could deal with that. I figured the DB would bump Skeets and eventually release him. Our rules dictate that if a defender is trailing a receiver, I just keep looking for the receiver because it's straight man-to-man coverage. If the defensive back is not running with the receiver, it's zone coverage.

What happened in this instance is the defender kept bumping Renaldo and pushed him down. He left Renaldo and was about 10 yards away from him as I threw a pass in Renaldo's direction. The defender was in a great position to get up a full head of steam and blast Skeets. That's exactly what he did. He came flying from the blind side and nailed Renaldo under the chin. I was scared. I immediately thought about the hit Oakland Raiders' defensive back Jack Tatum had put on Darryl Stingley. That tackle ended Stingley's career. I prayed that Skeets would not end up in a wheelchair for the rest of his life. Thank God he "only" suffered a concussion.

So we had something of a history with Atlanta, and we were keyed up. Our defense caused six turnovers and a blocked punt, leading to a 35–17 win. The following week we blew out Minnesota 51–7. Derrick Harmon, the running back who had ventured west to play for us out of Cornell University, and Billy Ring each scored a touchdown. I knew special things were happening. As we ran off the field, Bill had one of the biggest smiles on his face that I have ever seen, just like the one he had after we beat Cleveland.

Going into the last game against the Los Angeles Rams, we wanted to wrap it up and move on to the playoffs. We squeaked by the Rams 19–16, and became the NFL's first team to win fifteen games during the regular season.

Now it was time for the real season—the playoffs. We couldn't wait to get started, but unfortunately there was a two-week layoff because of the wild card games. If we were feeling cooped up, I imagined that our first opponents, the New York Giants, were feeling the walls closing in. After all, we had beaten them 31–10 way back on October 8. The Giants had something to prove, but we came out smoking. Everything that was pent up inside of the 49ers was released on our first possession of the game. We went 71 yards on eight plays to take a 7–0 lead. I hit D.C. with a 21-yard pass. Dwight ran into the Giants' left cornerback Kenny Daniel at the 10-yard line and cut sharply, angling to the post. This was a familiar Dwight Clark pass pattern. He caught the ball at the 2-yard line and went in for the score. The 49ers' adrenaline was flowing. We went right back, going 12 yards in two plays. Russ Francis took off on the right side of the line and was head to head with the Giants' inside linebacker Gary Reasons. Russ outmuscled Gary, and all of a sudden we were up 14–0 with only half the first quarter gone.

But with 8:12 left in the first quarter, our adrenaline started to evaporate. The 49ers were so psyched for the Giants we wanted to put them away early. This kind of mind-set can be dangerous. We had started so fast that we were faced with the situation of having to hang on. In the second quarter, with 11:34 left, the Giants went on an eleven-play drive covering 37 yards. The drive ended with Ali Haji-Sheikh, the Giants' field-goal kicker, nailing one from 46 yards out. The Giants came right back. I tried to throw from our end zone to Dwight, who was running a hook pattern on the left side of the field. Harry Carson got way up in the air, intercepted the ball out, and eased his way in for the score with 6:41 left in the half. We came back with 4:09 left. I play-faked on first down, froze the Giants' line-

backers, and made Terry Kinard hustle from his free-safety position to stop what he thought was a running play. While all this
was going on, Freddie Solomon faked Giants' cornerback Perry
Williams to the ouside and ran to the inside. I hit Fred for a 20-
yard touchdown. I had a lot of time to throw the ball, thanks to
Russ Francis, who put a great block on Lawrence Taylor on the
left side of our line. The half ended with the 49ers leading
21–10.

As I went into the locker room I realized we had expended
our adrenaline. I also realized we had the guts to hang on and
win the game. We had come so far that nothing was going to
stop us now.

In the second half we had trouble three minutes into the
third quarter. The 49ers had a first down at the Giants' 14-yard
line, when Wendell Tyler was thrown for a loss of 3 yards. On
the next play, I spotted Freddie standing alone in the end zone.
Damn it, I screwed up. Giants linebacker Gary Reasons intercepted my pass at the 3 and took it back 33 yards. Lawrence
Taylor hammered me on the play, and all I could so was sit on
the turf and pound my ankle with my fist. I was frustrated. We
had had a chance to go up 28–10 if I hadn't thrown that interception. Two plays before, I had run the ball down the left sideline to the Giants' 14-yard line. We were in a position to score
and I blew it. Yes, the run had taken a lot of wind out of me, but
that was no excuse. When a receiver is as wide open as Freddie
was it's my job to get the ball to him.

My long run took place on a crucial third-and-10 situation
on our 33-yard line. I saw Dwight running a hook pattern, but I
also saw a huge hole on the left side of the Giants' line. This was
no time for indecisiveness. I took off, and after picking up about
10 yards, I was ready to step out of bounds. However, two defenders ran by me, so I made an inside move, figuring—at the
least—I could drive out of bounds for the first down. But I kept
running. Suddenly I was all alone, all by myself. A quarterback's
dream come true. At the 14-yard line I ran out of bounds. I
couldn't catch my breath. I was thinking that the only time I'd
ever ran farther was when Mom was chasing me.

In the second half no one could score. We had our chances and so did the Giants. It's just one of those things. I give credit to both defenses. They worked their butts off, stopping each offense when it looked like they were on the brink of pushing it in. Lawrence Taylor was throwing his body all over the field; the man took no prisoners. Likewise did Ronnie Lott. Ronnie was starting for the first time since November 18, when he had dislocated his right shoulder on the first play from scrimmage against Tampa Bay. Against the Giants, Ronnie started at free safety but moved to cornerback in the second quarter when Dwight Hicks sprained his ankle.

Although we didn't murder the Giants, we put enough points on the board to win. Statistically, I even had a good day, completing twenty-five passes for 309 yards and carrying the ball three times for 63 yards. Normally, that kind of day would lead to a big win for the 49ers but the Giants were tough. At least we won. Our next stop was a date with the Chicago Bears and a matchup for the National Football Conference Championship.

We had revenge on our minds during our preparation for the Bears. Fourteen months ago, Thanksgiving weekend of 1983, the Bears had beaten us 13–3 at Soldiers Field on a typical cold, windy, icy Chicago afternoon. While they were beating us, their players were insulting us. After that game they issued some verbal cheap shots at our coaches.

Before the 1984 playoff game, they popped off again. The Bears said they would beat us, and then have themselves a nice time in San Francisco while they waited to take the field at Stanford Stadium, the home of Super Bowl XIX. Talk about putting the cart before the horse!

Of course we knew the Bears had a tremendous defense led by their defensive coach, Buddy Ryan, who is now the head coach of the Philadelphia Eagles. And then there was their intense head coach, Mike Ditka. He was in a strange situation. His offense was predictable; he had Walter Payton but nothing much else. His job had to be that of a motivator. Jim McMahon, the Bears' starting quarterback, was injured and wouldn't play.

This left Mike with Steve Fuller, who was a college teammate of Dwight Clark's at Clemson, to start in what was—at that point—the biggest game of Mike's coaching career.

We took the Bears' mouthing off in stride and let them do all the talking. Naturally, Chicago's defense was the guts of the team. In seventeen games, only four teams had rushed for over 100 yards against them. Our defense knew all about this and had a big surprise for the "Monsters of the Midway." All week before the game, Dwight Hicks, Keena Turner, and Ronnie Lott were talking shutout. They had something to prove. The media hyped Chicago's defense, but our hitmen knew they were better.

As far as I was concerned, my preparation centered on Chicago's defensive front. It's a funny-type front; they play eight men on the line of scrimmage and like to mix things up with a lot of stunting, twisting, and constant motion. This confused me because I didn't know which defender would be blitzing and which defender was going to drop back and cover our receivers. Despite their unique defense, the 49ers knew we could beat Chicago. Bill Walsh and Paul Hackett sat down with me and figured out that the way to attack their defense was to get our passes away super fast. We wouldn't look for big plays, just quick 4- or 5-yard passes. If this worked it would open up our running attack. And if we could keep the ball moving, our offense would likely be able to throw the Chicago defense off stride. The coaches also decided to attack the Bears with full blitz protection on every play. If Chicago's eight-man front didn't come with an all-out blitz, our backs would release and run a short-pass pattern. If I saw that the Bears weren't going to use an eight-man front, I would audible.

As we all studied films of the Bears' defense the week before the game, we discovered certain tendencies we could exploit. For example, Bobb saw that Mike Hartenstine, Chicago's right defensive end, wouldn't be able to tackle any of our backs because he played too wide. None of the Bears' previous opponents took advantage of that tendency.

Then it was time to play. In the locker room I was looking

forward to getting on the field. At the same time I was nervous. I was quite aware of what the Bears' defense had done to teams throughout the season; they literally tore people up. My concern wasn't for my physical well-being; it was the fact that I wanted to play a perfect game. My next thought was "God, it's almost impossible to achieve perfection against any team." As I walked through the tunnel and heard the 61,040 fans pouring their hearts out, one thing went through my mind. I was going to put my faith in my brothers up front, our offensive line—Paris, Ayers, Quillan, Cross, and Fahnhorst. They would give me the time to get rid of the ball. These gentlemen had a score to settle with the Bears and I felt their confidence. They were conscious about protecting me, but that came second to them. Their major concern was preventing Chicago from breaking them down, not letting the Bears rip our offense apart the way they had other teams during the season. The 49ers' offensive line was mentally set. Pride was their catalyst. Even though I made mistakes during our first two offensive series, I knew we had things under control. We moved the ball at will and the Bears' defense couldn't stop us. We took Chicago out of their normal tendencies and were on our way to a win.

Moe gave us the lead, kicking a 21-yard field goal. We moved the ball 73 yards in nine plays. I hit Freddie with an 11-yard pass that moved the ball to our 34-yard line. Then I hooked up with D.C. for 38 yards, putting us in Bears' territory at their 28-yard line. Renaldo got into the act by catching a 10-yard pass at the Chicago 17. Freddie pulled in a 12-yard pass, putting the 49ers deep in Chicago territory at the 5. We didn't score a touchdown but we were moving the ball rapidly. With a first and goal at the 5-yard line and second and goal at the 2, I threw a pass away, then I fumbled Fred Quillan's snap on third down. I was trying to do too much on the fumble. As I backed away from Fred, I tried to read the defense at the same time. Luckily, I fell on the ball. I was so close to scoring twice I was feeling frustrated. At least by falling on the ball I was preserving Moe's field goal. We hung tough and didn't panic. We were moving the ball and it was only a matter of time before we would break the game open.

Despite my mistakes, Chicago's defense was on the run. They had not experienced this type of ball movement, this kind of domination, all season. We were moving the ball at will. On the first drive I completed five out of seven passes. When I went to the bench, I wasn't surprised how easily we moved down the field because our offensive line achieved their goal; they broke the Bears' defense.

Meanwhile, our defense did what they had quietly talked about the week before the game. They dominated the Bears' offense throughout the game, holding Steve Fuller to a total of 87 yards passing and sacking him nine times. They also held Walter Payton to 92 yards. Walter's longest run was 20 yards.

Everyone was playing as if his life depended on this game. This was a direct result of the Chicago players' putting us down. We were so keyed up I got the distinct feeling we actually won the game in the second quarter. We were executing Bill's game plan to perfection.

However, in the first quarter I also negotiated a drive that ended in an interception. With a first and goal on the 2, I threw a lightweight pass that Gary Fencik picked off. My mistake was that I saw Gary moving toward Freddie, who was wide open. I just released a soft pass instead of stepping up in the pocket and firing the ball. This error wasn't fatal, because our defense was making life miserable for Chicago's offense. During six consecutive early possessions, the 49ers' defense didn't let Chicago out of its own half of the field. The only crack the Bears got at a score was a 41-yard field-goal attempt that Bob Thomas kicked wide to the right.

Early in the second quarter, Bill put the psych to work, trying to rattle the Bears' cage. With a first and 10 at the Chicago 32, I lined up at quarterback but suddenly exchanged places with Freddie. I was our right end and Freddie was the 49ers' quarterback. I was face to face with Todd Bell, who normally plays strong safety but changed positions because cornerback

Terry Schmidt was out with a bruised thigh. Freddie took the snap from Fred Quillan and ran a veer option. He pitched to Roger Craig, who was stopped for no gain. Meanwhile, I was lined up nose to nose with Todd, and he was definitely surprised. As soon as the ball was snapped, I was to turn tail and run the other way. We didn't expect to gain anything on the play. It was designed to make Chicago think, get them talking and thinking about what we might try next.

Todd was selected to the Pro Bowl that year and so was I. He told me if I had lined up against him again he would have flat-out punched me as hard as he could. Actually, we were thinking of running the play in the first quarter but I didn't like the defensive set and audibled into another play.

After Bob Thomas missed the field goal, we went on another long drive that ended with Moe kicking a 22-yard field goal. Dana McLemore got things started by returning a Chicago punt 25 yards and I went to work. We marched 65 yards on twelve plays. I hooked up with Freddie for a 12-yard gain, moving us to our own 43-yard line. Then I found Freddie again for 15 yards, taking us to the Chicago 45-yard line. Moving right along, I spotted D.C. at the Chicago 18. Then it was back to Freddie, putting us at the Bears' 4-yard line. Once again, we couldn't score a touchdown. Roger Craig was stopped after a 1-yard gain; Wendell Tyler was hit by Richard Dent and lost 2 yards; and Dan Hampton batted away my pass. Moe kicked the field goal and we were up 6–0 at the end of the first half. It was really frustrating. On that particular drive, I hit on four of six passes for 56 yards and only came away with 3 points. Well, at least we were ahead and had given the Bears' defense more than they could handle.

There was another positive sign. I had time to throw the ball because our running game was working. Although we only had 43 yards rushing in the first half, it was enough to keep the Bears' defense on guard. The previous week, in their first playoff game against the Washington Redskins, Joe Theismann had passed seventeen consecutive times. The Redskins couldn't generate a running attack. Once the Bears realized this, they could dig in and turn my fellow Notre Dame alumnus into a human punching bag. The Bears didn't have to guess. They knew the only way Theismann could beat them was to pass, pass, pass. Although we were only ahead 6–0 at the half, we were moving the ball against Chicago. I knew our defensive coordinator, George Seifert, had to be pleased. We kept the pressure off of our defense. The "D" spent a lot of time on the sidelines resting. When they came into the game they were fresh and able to put maximum pressure on Chicago.

We hit a very high level of confidence as we click-clacked through the tunnel for the second half. We got off to a quick start. The defense and special teams took control of the game, delivering their form of a boxer's knockout punch. Our punter, Max Runager, got off a 41-yard sky job that Chicago couldn't return. Steve Fuller called on Payton three straight times from the Chicago 11-yard line. It just wasn't meant to be. Our defense got nasty. Walter—known to fans and players as "Sweetness"—carried the load for the Bears the entire game and could only gain 1 yard, forcing Chicago to punt from deep in their own territory. Chicago's punter, Dave Finzer—who had punted seven times for a 43-yard average—was faced with a fourth and 9 at his own 12-yard line. Dave had to be feeling queasy; after all, our special team could take that sprinter's stance, and put on a double-time rush. Dave came through, nailing his punt to midfield, but Dana McLemore ran the ball back to the Bears' 35-yard line. There was no doubt in my mind that Bill would go to the running game. Wendell Tyler had runs of 11 and 5 yards. On his 11-yard run, we caught a major break. Dave Duerson was penalized for illegal contact. We were positioned at the Chicago 9-yard line, rather than a third and 5 at the Chicago 14-yard line.

We had to score a touchdown in order to put the Bears away. If we had come this close to the end zone without getting 6 points, the Bears might have had a chance to get back into the game. With the football resting at the 9-yard line, Bill sent in the "Angus" formation. Guy McIntyre, a six-foot-three, 271-pound guard from the University of Georgia who was in his rookie season, came into the game and lined up in the fullback slot. He would act as a blocking back for Wendell. The play was named after the Black Angus restaurant in Redwood City, where Guy would occasionally eat during his rookie season.

Guy got a running start and blocked Dan Hampton, taking him out of the play. Wendell broke two tackles on his way to the 49ers' first touchdown of the game. I was not only relieved that we had scored but happy for Wendell. I knew the Bears wanted to force him to fumble in a key situation but they couldn't do it. Their frustration showed when at one point during the third quarter they asked the referees to check and see if Wendell had any stickum—which is illegal—on his hands. It was hard for the Bears to believe that he was holding on to the ball.

The fourth quarter began with the 49ers up 13 points. I knew we needed just one more score to put the game out of reach. Chicago couldn't generate any offense and another 49er touchdown would likely demoralize them. I got the feeling the Bears' defense was tired; they were dragging. We had kept them moving all afternoon and now was the time to deliver the final blow.

Moving from our own 12-yard line, I rolled out and hit Mike Wilson—our wide receiver—who took the ball to our 25. Then it was another quick pass to Wendell, and he ran the ball close to midfield. At this point the 49ers pulled off a big play. I handed the ball to Roger, who ran to his left. The side was cleared for him on great blocks by tight end John Frank and guard John Ayers. The Bears finally caught Roger at their 14-yard line. Two plays later I went looking for Freddie. The play was similar to the catch Dwight had made against Dallas to win the NFC title in 1982. Bears' safety Dave Duerson was blitzing, so I rolled out to my right to get away from him. Freddie was supposed to run an "out" pattern, but when he came off the line of scrimmage, Bears cornerback Mike Richardson jumped to

Freddie's outside. As I was moving to my right, I saw Freddie run to the inside and stop. I knew he was going to pivot and execute a spinning move. He then ran to the outside corner of the end zone. I just let the ball go to that outside spot and Casper was there, pulling the ball in for a 10-yard touchdown that would make it impossible for Chicago to come back. There was still 11:55 left in the game, but it was over as far as I was concerned. The San Francisco 49ers were going to the Super Bowl for the second time in four years.

We scored one more time when Moe kicked another field goal, making the score 23–0. We had dominated the media-darling Bears' defense and our workmanlike defense came out of the game as the true stars—the no-nonsense hitmen. The one memory from the game that still sticks in my mind was standing next to Ronnie Lott on the sidelines during the final seconds and grabbing his hand. The expression on Ronnie's face could have lit up San Francisco. The 49ers had come such a long way from that defeat in Washington one year ago in Washington, and Ronnie knew it. Mr. Lott would rest well that night; we had come all the way back from frustration and weren't going to be stopped. The 49ers were ready for Dan Marino and Don Shula's Miami Dolphins.

I knew exactly who the media was going to be talking about during Super Bowl XIX—Dan Marino. After all, Danny had thrown fifty-five touchdown passes in eighteen games and I hadn't exactly set the world on fire during the playoffs. But I knew we had the better all-around team. We proved we were the best-balanced team in the National Football League during the 1984 season. After all, we only lost one game during the regular season and playoffs. Miami was coming into the Super Bowl with a 16-2 record. If the press wanted to concentrate on Danny it was fine with me. The less pressure the better.

The 49ers were used to this kind of treatment from the media in 1984. They said we didn't have a tough schedule, they said we were lucky to get through the playoffs, and finally, they believed the Bears' defense was going to tear us up. I've learned that you have to believe in yourself. We knew what we could do and I suspected the Dolphins knew they were going to be involved with the best team in the NFL, despite what anyone was saying.

We had a couple of distinct advantages going into the Super Bowl. First, we were no strangers to championship games, the coaches knew what to expect, and Jerry Walker, our director of public relations, knew just how to handle the media, how to make things easy for us so we could concentrate on the game. Second, we were playing what was virtually a home game. Stanford Stadium, located in Palo Alto, was about an hour and a half from San Francisco. As I said before, simulating home-game practice and game conditions is important. Bill let us live in our own homes, while the Dolphins had to spend ten days in a strange hotel. We were relaxed and in a familiar atmosphere. I was able to go through the same routine I did during home games all season. When a team is on the road for ten days it's natural for them to want to go out exploring, especially in a beautiful San Francisco. We had already seen the sights and eaten in the fine restaurants many times. We were able to concentrate on one thing—the Super Bowl.

Despite this relaxed atmosphere, I began feeling pressure during the second week leading up to the game. I never thought about Danny and the comparisons that sportswriters were making during the regular season. The only thought going through my mind was tremendous respect for this man who was playing to perfection. He was carrying the Miami Dolphins—not only carrying them but doing it with a banged-up knee.

The press misread my quiet nature. Some even resorted to calling me a "wimp." They would ask me questions like "Joe, Marino's had such a great season, how are you going to stop him?"

"Fellows, you're talking to the wrong guy. I don't have to stop Dan, our defense does, and they've been having a great year. You agree with that, don't you?" My answer was met with stone silence. I wondered why they weren't asking the key question: How was Miami's offense going to score on our defense? If they had taken the time to look back on our 17-1 season they would have realized we had the best "D" in football. Why didn't they ask who was going to stop our offense? No one, with the exception of Pittsburgh, had been able to. Our accomplishments were being totally ignored. My main concern was that the press not draw me into a duel with Danny. If they did, it would extend to the field and force me out of my game. Dan can hit long and quickly. Hell, if anyone took the time to look back at the 1981–82 season, when we won the first Super Bowl, they would realize that I too had a lot of success throwing long. Things had changed: Now we relied on the balance between our short passing game and Roger and Wendell running the ball. As it got closer to the game, a lot of people took shots at us. Even Al Davis, the managing general partner of the Los Angeles Raiders, got into the act. He said I was a "drifter, not a great scrambler." He also said I couldn't throw deep to the sidelines. Al said I had the ability to destroy the morale of a defensive football team by my "great consistency of percentage throwing." All I could do was laugh. Everyone had an opinion, everyone was trying to get into the Super Bowl act.

A few days before the game I was feeling not only pressure but anger. The Marino thing was part of the buildup. Although I was dying inside having to be questioned about Danny at every press conference, I could live with that. The 1984 season had been incredibly good for the 49ers and for me personally. Our season was excellent, and during '84 I had also put personal problems behind me. Divorce is never easy, and mine had been played out in public. But the whole thing was behind me now, and Jennifer and I were looking forward to getting married. I came out of my personal problem with some semblance of sanity. I realized it was imperative for me to transfer my decisiveness on the field to my life away from football.

But on this cool Sunday in January, I wasn't thinking about my own problems. For one of the few times in my career I was angry. Angry at people who said I didn't compare with Dan

Marino. Angry at people who didn't give our defense—anchored by Ronnie Lott, Hacksaw Reynolds, and Keena Turner—a hell of a lot of credit. Angry at Doug Betters, a defensive lineman who was sitting in the opponents' locker room thinking about putting a hurt on me. Little did he know I considered him overrated, an average player on a mediocre defense. This was the guy who, two weeks before the Super Bowl, told the world that Joe Montana was only interested in money. He used the Super Bowl buildup to tell a group of reporters that, because I wouldn't get paid, I had refused to make a personal appearance on behalf of the Special Olympics in his home state of Montana.

No one needs a reason to get up for the Super Bowl. But Betters made me feel like I was fighting for my life. I didn't respond to him at first because I wasn't sure what he was talking about. But when I went back and looked at my schedule for that period, I found out that I was appearing somewhere else, a commitment I had made months in advance. Why would he say this? It made me believe that the Dolphins—as a team—and Betters, as an individual, weren't too sure of themselves. If Betters thought he had to manufacture a story to give his team some kind of a psychological lift, they were in deep trouble. Maybe they were a little scared of us. "This can't be," I told Jennifer. "I thought they had more confidence in themselves."

The Friday night before the game we had a little time to ourselves. I knew the team hotel—the Amfac, near the airport—would be a madhouse, so Jennifer and I decided to have dinner at my cousin Michael's place, a two-bedroom condominium where we'd stayed during the playoffs. Mike is an air-traffic controller in San Francisco. My first experiences in football were with him as midget leaguers in Pennsylvania. He also shared an apartment with me in South Bend during my senior year at Notre Dame.

I thought his place would be a good spot to relax for a while before I checked into the hotel. Was I wrong! We were there by ourselves until Mike came back with a lot of the family, who he had been entertaining downtown. My mom and dad came and Jen's family was there. All of a sudden the party of two was a party of twenty-two. The family was excited. They wanted autographs and pictures and I was just trying to take it easy two nights before the Super Bowl. Normally, I would have loved to be with them and done anything they wanted. But at that point, Joe Cool was Mr. Nervous. It was about time to check into the hotel and I kept looking at the clock. Everyone was being so nice but all this was driving me crazy. I went into another room and began packing my bag to leave for the hotel. I was trying to open a sliding-glass mirrored closet door to get something. I was about to tear it apart because it wouldn't move. I was slamming it, jamming it, shaking the damn thing. Jennifer came in. "Joe, I'll do it," she said. A flick of the wrist and it was opened, and we just about ran out of there. Impolite? Maybe, but they understood. I needed her to get me out of there. The crazies definitely had set in. I wanted finally to hit the field.

The locker room at Stanford Stadium provided me with the first bit of calm I'd felt in four months. The 1985 Super Bowl was only a couple of hours away, but for me the locker room was an isle of tranquillity. There was no other place I'd rather be. The atmosphere wasn't much different than that on an average game day. After all, a lot of us had been to the Super Bowl in '82. But this was different. As I said, no one had given us any respect in '84. No respect from the media—so what else is new in San Francisco?—no respect from our opponents, and even some of our fans doubted us because we didn't totally destroy the New York Giants in the playoffs. They also wondered why we didn't look sharp against the Chicago Bears in the NFC Championship game. Leave it to Bill to calm his team down. He was lying on a bag of equipment, thinking out loud. "All they can talk about is Miami's offense. What about our defense? All they can talk about is Marino, Marino, Marino. We have some guys who can play too."

Sometimes it's hard to tell with Bill. He could have been trying to psych us, or he could have just been releasing tension. Whatever his motive, it was working, because everyone heard him.

It was time to head to the field for warmups. There's no feeling like going on the field in a Super Bowl game, but this time it was really special. We were playing in front of a home crowd in Palo Alto. As Matt Cavanaugh and I ran up the ramp leading onto the field with the trainers, people were giving me the thumbs-up sign. We looked back at the video screens near the scoreboard. They were playing a public-service commercial I had done for the United Way. Tony Bennett was singing "I Left My Heart in San Francisco." The crowd went crazy and goose bumps began forming on my neck. It was finally time to play football.

When I stepped on the field for our first series of plays, I lost control. All the pent-up anger I had walked around with the week before the game was released by getting out of our game plan. On our first play I threw long down the sideline when I should have hit Freddie, who was running a short pattern. Then I tried throwing long down the middle to Renaldo. When I came back to the bench Paul was on the phone.

"What the hell are you doing?" he said. "We haven't practiced those plays all week."

"You're crazy," I said. "They [the Dolphins] were in the right coverage for us to throw long. We practiced throwing the post [pattern] down the middle, I just didn't throw it right!"

"Joe, just settle down and play your game instead of trying to push the ball down the field and make the one big play," Paul said. "You're trying to play Marino's game."

Dan and the Dolphins came right out and did just what they had been doing all season; they took the ball down the field in a hurry, using a no-huddle offense. Miami moved 45 yards in seven plays. The drive ended with a 37-yard field goal by Uwe von Schamann. Midway through that drive—the fourth play, to be exact—a key defensive adjustment by the 49ers took place. We switched to our "elephant" defense, the creation of our defensive coordinator, George Seifert. The "elephant" meant that

Hacksaw Reynolds came out for a fourth defensive lineman and Mike Walter replaced weak-side linebacker Dan Bunz. George told me that when the Dolphins started the no-huddle offense, our defense went to the nickel defense because it's much more flexible and can stop runs. The nickel stopped the no-huddle offense. George also used a lot more man-to-man coverage than we usually do. Jeff Fuller played a key role in the game. Jeff is our whip linebacker. The whip means a combination linebacker/safety. It gave the 49ers a lot of flexibility when it came to coverage and blitzing.

After my chat with Paul we went into high gear. I knew we had to do two things: regain the momentum and return to our own style of play. I realized we had to score a touchdown 49ers style. That meant pushing down the field by controlling the ball. We went 78 yards in eight plays before I rolled out and found Carl Monroe for the touchdown.

The Dolphins came right back to score when Dan hit his tight end Dan Johnson with a 2-yard pass for a score. The Dolphins moved right down the field in six plays. The big plays were an 18-yard pass to Mark Clayton and a 21-yard pass to Johnson. During the second quarter the 49ers took over the game, scoring three times. On our first drive, Roger Craig, who would wind up having a tremendous day—58 yards rushing, 82 yards receiving—scored from 8 yards out to end a 47-yard drive. We pushed the ball down the field using short passes, but I noticed something in the Miami defense that I would take advantage of most of the afternoon. I knew Miami's linebackers were turning away from me as they dropped behind to cover our backs, who were running patterns out of the backfield. I just moved out of the pocket and followed their linebackers down the field. How could they tackle me? They were running downfield. On Roger's score I was able to use this tactic for a 19-yard run. We continued to use our short passing game the rest of the first half and went ahead 28–16 at the half.

The 49ers put the game away in the third quarter. We scored twice; Moe kicked a field goal, and I hooked up with

Roger for a 16-yard touchdown pass. It was 38–10, and there was no way Miami was coming back. Our defense was amazing. Although Danny completed twenty-nine out of fifty passes for 318 yards, the Miami offense couldn't go anywhere. Dan was sacked four times—the most he had been sacked all year—and intercepted twice. I threw for 331 yards and ran for 59.

Yes, I finally felt vindicated. I was voted MVP of the game, but in reality, I knew the 49ers played a perfect football game. Not only did the defense frustrate and dominate the Dolphins but our offense scored on five consecutive possessions in the second and third quarters.

I didn't get much sleep after the game. There was reason to celebrate. I just had one piece of missing business to attend to. As I walked my mom and dad through the San Francisco airport the day after the game, we kept talking about the win. As we approached the gate I slipped off my first Super Bowl ring and gave it to Dad. He put his arms around me and I thought I saw a tear roll down his cheek. We had come a long way from those Mon City days.

1986: Oh My Aching Back!
To Repeat or Not Repeat

Going into our 1985 training camp, I was experiencing severe lower-back pain. The stiffness prevented me from loosening up thoroughly. Although I wasn't physically sound, I didn't pay any attention to my condition or really worry about it.

For most of my career I've lived with aches and pains; this isn't unusual for most NFL quarterbacks. We all deal with pain in one form or another, and it usually recurs in the same area. Like a nagging toothache that won't go away, it bothers a quarterback on and off during his career and is something we each learn to live with and play through. In my case, it's a sciatic-nerve problem. It surprises me because I never know when it's going to surface.

I was faced with a serious injury following our win over the Bengals in the 1982 Super Bowl. My knee had been bothering me all season but I put off any type of surgery because the pain wasn't serious. But when the season ended I had to undergo knee surgery, something I'd never experienced before. When I realized a doctor was going to cut into my knee, I was concerned and nervous about it. A number of considerations passed through my mind, the major one being if I blew out my knee my career would likely be over just months after we'd won the Super Bowl.

The procedure I underwent to determine what was wrong with my knee is called arthroscopic surgery. It was a quick operation. The physician made a tiny incision in my knee and injected a dye in the hole to locate the problem. It didn't take long to find some torn cartilage and remove it—about a half hour. I was fortunate. My game is based on quickness. If I had lost my mobility I would have been in big trouble. The rehabilitation process wasn't extensive. I worked out on a machine that allowed me to add different weights to strengthen my leg.

From then on I was fine, until my 1985 preseason back problem. I just didn't feel right. I'd aggravated my back when I left Rocklin one weekend to move furniture into our home in Redwood City. I didn't want to leave Jennifer alone to take care of moving the furniture. She was pregnant and couldn't really move a lot of furniture around.

I realized the seriousness of my back problem during a preseason game with the Denver Broncos. Dan Reeves, the Broncos' head coach, was going all out, as if it were a regular-season game. He used his starters throughout the game. Perhaps this was a sign of things to come for the 49ers. During the 1985 season, everyone approached us with tremendous intensity. They all wanted a piece of the Super Bowl champions. I knew Bill was mad at Dan for leaving his starters in during a meaningless exhibition game, but Bill kept his feelings to himself. His strategy during the preseason is to show our opponents absolutely nothing. Why waste our regular-season strategy?

With the Bronco starters still in the game, Bill casually looked back at his first team. "Would anyone like to go back into the game?" he asked, with a smile on his face. We all understood the meaning of Bill's quip. I had twisted my back badly early in the game. I was scrambling to my right and I just twisted very hard in that direction as I threw the football.

When I released the ball I heard something pop and felt the pain immediately. What had originally been a stiff back suddenly became a severely strained back. The pain was so bad that I couldn't practice the following week. The day we broke camp, I was in the doctor's office undergoing a CAT scan on my back. The CAT-scan machine examined and took close-up pictures of my spine. Not only did I have scoliosis, or swayback, but the CAT scan revealed that my vertebra was twisted. The stiffness I experienced in training camp combined with the pop in the Denver game caused a serious problem. Swayback is something I've lived with for a long time. The 49ers' physician, Dr. Michael Dillingham, told me the problem was congenital.

It didn't affect my throwing motion but it scared me. One treatment that was prescribed was spending a lot of time in the swimming pool at Rocklin. The water workout, designed by Jerry Attaway, the 49ers' conditioning coach, consisted of walking laps with Matt Cavanaugh back and forth in the pool. We wore jackets around our waists that kept us afloat. The workout not only relaxed my lower back but it also increased my wind and strengthened my heart muscles. A number of 49ers were undergoing the same treatment. Defensive end Fred Dean, who underwent a knee operation during the off-season, spent a lot of time floating with the jacket in the pool. Moe also walked laps with me.

For social relaxation, Bill set up a fishing contest following our first exhibition victory over the Los Angeles Raiders. He got the idea from Bubba Paris, who spotted some bluegills and stepped into a small man-made pond to catch them. Bill stocked the pond with catfish and organized teams. We all fished in half-hour shifts. My team came in last, catching forty-nine fish. The winning team won $100 per man and the man who caught the biggest fish—Dan Huey, a rookie wideout who didn't make the team—won $100. Of course, Bubba, "Mr. Fisherman," tried playing all the angles. He sprayed his bait with some kind of mystical formula, but it didn't work too well.

The next night Bill arranged a trip for the team to the Cal

Expo in Sacramento to take in a Huey Lewis and the News concert. Although Huey is one of my favorite singers, I was just too tired to go.

Immediately after the CAT scan, I was out for two weeks—missing the final two exhibition games—and I was driving everyone crazy. I hung around PR head Jerry Walker's office, and drove him crazy. Jerry couldn't wait for me to go back to work. To say that I was anxious to get back on the field was an understatement. I tried to watch practice but I couldn't. Every time Matt completed a pass I cringed; I guess it was that competitive feeling.

On September 2, I returned to practice and my timing was way off. It really bothered me. I began to press because my receivers deserved better. Even though we were just practicing they were frustrated. Freddie, Dwight, and Jerry Rice, who was in his first season with the team, were trying to get ready for the season and I was throwing the ball eight feet behind them.

Throughout the rest of training camp and during the season, I received back treatment. I started feeling better after a while, and the treatment was primarily a precautionary measure. Our trainers would turn my body at a 45-degree angle and rock me. I also did press-ups. Despite my problems I thought the 49ers were ready for another run at the Super Bowl. The more people doubted we'd repeat as Super Bowl champs, the more we wanted to prove them wrong. The team was looking forward to the season; we were still having fun playing football.

I knew the first game was going to be a physical test for me. I felt fine but I knew the test would come when one of the Minnesota Vikings delivered a hit to my back. We got off to a fast start against the Vikes. After Dwaine Board, our defensive end, recovered a fumble deep in Minnesota territory, I hit Roger with a short pass that he carried to the 10-yard line. Then Roger ran the ball into the end zone, giving us a quick 7–0 lead. I was feeling OK but I knew I looked stiff. It had nothing to do with my back; I was just pressing too hard and not relaxing. On our second possession, I threw a pass that flew over our bench. The pass made me conscious of how I was throwing the ball. Dwight was open on the play, and Russ Francis was also open shorter, which would have been an easier throw. Bill had a few words with me. I could tell he was mad and I started pressing even harder.

During our third drive we moved the ball well. As it turned out, the drive would also turn into the physical test I was waiting for. We moved from our own 7-yard line to the Vikings' 22. With a third and 8 I saw an opening and ran with the ball. When I started running I figured I would just run out of bounds, but one of the Vikings' linebackers was near the sideline and I wouldn't have made it. What the heck. I tried running past the first-down marker. Scott Studwell, Minnesota's intense inside linebacker, closed in on me, and I dove for the first down as he blasted me. It looked like I was hurt because I couldn't get up. I was fine, I just couldn't catch my breath. When our trainers came out to attend to me I couldn't answer them so they thought I was hurt. Bill took me out of the game. Matt came in, and we moved to the 47-yard line before we had to punt the ball away. I came back in the game for what would turn out to be the start of several turnovers that eventually cost us the game.

Roger Craig had the ball stolen by Rufus Best, wiping out a gain that took the ball to the Viking 23. I had a pass intercepted by Mark Mullaney, a defensive lineman, in Minnesota territory, and Wendell fumbled the ball inside the Vikings' 10-yard line. The half ended with the 49ers leading 7–0, but the three turnovers, in all probability, kept us from scoring. Our luck didn't change in the second half. In the third quarter, with a second and goal inside the Minnesota 10, I hit Freddie Solomon with a pass but he fumbled the ball. Again the Vikings couldn't capitalize, but they were still very much in the game. On our next drive we moved from our 16-yard line to Minnesota's 45. With fourth and about an inch, Bill elected to have us punt.

Minnesota came back to score, and it was 7–7 with 1:01 left

in the third quarter. We went on an eight-play, 70-yard drive highlighted by a great leaping catch over the middle by our rookie wide receiver Jerry Rice. Jerry showed everyone that he wasn't afraid to go across the middle—the most dangerous spot for a receiver—to catch a pass. I try not to throw the ball in that spot to any receiver but I felt great knowing that "World" would go anywhere to catch one of my passes. Roger caught a pass for an 18-yard touchdown, putting us up 14–7 early in the fourth quarter. The Vikings tied the score on their next possession when Tommy Kramer connected with Mike Jones for a 44-yard touchdown pass. Roger put us ahead, scoring from 19 yards out, but the Vikings again took advantage of a turnover. Studwell knocked the ball out of Wendell Tyler's hands at our own 26-yard line. The Vikings quickly tied the game 21–21.

On the Vikings' kickoff Derrick Harmon fumbled and the Vikings recovered around our 20-yard line. Ted Brown ran the ball in for Minnesota, giving them a 28–21 win. We did have a chance for one more drive. We moved the ball from our own 29-yard line but were hurt by incomplete passes, dropped passes, and finally, a holding penalty that took us out of scoring range.

At the time we didn't know it, but this game was one of six frustrating losses we would suffer in 1985. We lost the six games by a total of 36 points. The Chicago Bears, who eventually won the '86 Super Bowl, beat us by 16 points. Besides that game, the largest margin of victory by an opponent was 7 points.

In the Minnesota game, not only did we have all the fumbles but some bad luck. I mean how often is a quarterback going to have a pass intercepted by a defensive lineman? Fortunately, the Vikings didn't turn Mullaney's interception into a score. In retrospect, the loss really put a lot of pressure on the 49ers because the Vikings were a team we should have beaten. We had 500 yards in total offense and still lost the game. Something is wrong when that happens. Not only did we begin putting pressure on ourselves but once again the newspapers started asking their favorite question: "What's wrong with the 49ers?" This time the writers had something to write about.

We won the next three out of four games—we lost 20–17 to New Orleans—and went into the Bears' game with a 3-2 record. The week prior to the Chicago game we had beaten Atlanta 38–17. I had a good game, completing thirty-seven passes for 429 yards and five touchdowns. But Chicago was undefeated, and as sure as I was that this was a key game for us—a loss would put us three games behind the Rams in the NFC West—I also knew the Bears would be coming to Candlestick looking to avenge their 23–0 playoff loss to us in January. The Chicago defense had been tearing teams up. We had to play a virtually mistake-free game. The key to beating the Bears was to get ahead of them early.

Unfortunately, it was the Bears' offense that put us in the hole. Chicago quarterback Jim McMahon passed on the Bears' first five plays and went 73 yards, ending in a 3-yard touchdown run by Walter Payton. The drive took just over two minutes. The next time they got the ball Chicago kicked a field goal. Their defense then caused two straight turnovers that resulted in two more field goals, giving them a 16–0 lead. The Bears' defense had us where they wanted us but we weren't going to give up. Our defense scored a touchdown when Todd Shell blitzed McMahon, who threw the ball right into Carlton Williamson's hands. Carlton ran the ball back, cutting the Chicago lead to 16–7. Late in the quarter we put a drive together, setting up a field goal that left us behind 16–10 at the end of the first half.

In the second half Chicago's defense began pressuring me up the middle. It was hard to see anything. We got in a lot of third-and-long situations. We managed only three first downs and 45 yards of offense in the second half. I couldn't get anything going and was sacked seven times. Although we were in the game early, Chicago dominated us in the second half and won 26–10. A little sidelight to the game: As the clock ran out on us, Mike Ditka put his 310-pound defensive lineman William

Perry in at the fullback position. He carried the ball twice for short gains. I guess this was Mike's answer to Bill using Guy McIntyre in the Angus formation during the playoff. If I know Bill, he'll have an answer for Mike when we play the Bears again.

We lost three more games—including a 7-point loss to the Rams that gave them the NFC West title—but none was as frustrating as a Monday night 17–16 loss in Denver to the Broncos. Not only was there a questionable interference call on Dwight Hicks but Moe missed a short field goal when Matt Cavanaugh, who is the holder on field goal and point after touchdown attempts, was distracted before placing the ball down. A fan threw a snowball at him. The thing that bothered me most about the snowball incident was that it wasn't unique; their fans had been throwing things at us all during the game. The snowball thrown at Matt just happened at a crucial time. I heard that the referees had warned the Broncos about the fans well before Moe's field-goal attempt but evidently no one cared. So many fans were throwing things at me that I didn't know whether I was getting hit with cups of ice or snowballs.

It reminded me of a similar situation my senior year at Notre Dame when we went to Atlanta to play Georgia Tech; the only difference was we were beating Tech. Their students were throwing objects at us the minute our buses pulled onto their campus. They were throwing everything from dead fish to champagne bottles. Jeff Weston, one of our players, picked up one of the bottles and almost went up into the stands with it looking to crack a few heads. After that, our whole team huddled on the field to decide whether we were going to stay and finish the game or leave. We decided to stay.

We played as hard as we could against Denver and lost. The snowball was distracting, but I've learned that anything can happen in the NFL. Four weeks later, the Rams clinched the NFC West, beating us 27–20 in San Francisco. This followed our pattern of frustration in '85. They tied the game 20–20 when Dwight Hicks and Ronnie Lott both tipped a Dieter

Brock pass into the hands of Henry Ellard for a touchdown. The Rams scored the winning touchdown when I attempted to pass over the middle to Carl Monroe. The ball was tipped right into the hands of Ram's defensive back Gary Green, who ran it back for a touchdown. With 1:55 left in the game, I was sacked and Gary Jeter recovered my fumble, ensuring the Rams' win.

We had to win our next two games to get a wild card spot in the playoffs. We went to New Orleans and beat the Saints 31–19, and in our final game of the regular season beat the Cowboys in Candlestick 31–16. This sent us on a coast-to-coast flight to New Jersey to play the Giants. I had taken a rough physical beating during the season, ending with a pulled abdominal muscle on my left side during the Cowboys' game. It was really difficult throwing the ball early in the week during our preparation for the Giants. I also had a cold, and when I coughed or sneezed it killed me. The pain was very bad but I didn't want to take any shots because I don't like needles. I can't stand the feeling of a needle going into my body, so I usually avoid any kind of shot as long as possible. I'm also aware that there can be severe aftereffects from any kind of pain killer. I asked Dr. Dillingham if the shots could hurt me.

"You could take them and try to block out the pain or play without them," he said. "Either way you might tear the muscle a little more but it is so bad now, I don't think it can get any worse."

I trust Dr. Dillingham and decided to take the pain killers. I had eight injections between the Wednesday before the Giants game and game time. One important factor usually works in my favor when I'm dealing with pain. When I go out on the field, my adrenaline really starts flowing. It blocks out any pain naturally. This, combined with the shots, convinced me that I would be able to play against the Giants.

The night before the game I had some Mexican food—a couple of tacos and an enchilada—with my parents and their friends in the team's hotel. Just being around my folks and their friends was relaxing; it made me feel a lot better. After dinner I went to our team meeting then went to my room, took a sleeping pill, and watched some basketball with Dwight Clark.

It was kind of funny: I was experiencing this pain on the eve of a big game and all I could think about was Jen and the Pumpkin. I called Larry Muno just to tell him how I was feeling but spent most of the time on the telephone with his little son Christopher. Now you know what a quarterback does for fun the night before a playoff game! The next day I was feeling all right. When I stepped on the field at 11 A.M. with Matt, Dwight, and Freddie I was greeted by boos and insults. The Giants fans, or should I say fanatics, are a wild and faithful bunch. They're a lot like our fans. The 49ers had the Giants' number going back to 1982 when we beat them in the playoffs on our way to the Super Bowl. The insults were wide-ranging. I hear the same "clever" lines wherever we play.

Even though the 49ers were banged up, we believed we had a shot at returning to the Super Bowl. But in reality we were a wounded team. Randy Cross didn't play, Roger Craig was hurting, and you know how I felt. The Giants' defense took advantage of our condition. They contained me so I couldn't scramble throughout the game; consequently, I had to throw short passes all day. They also put a tail on Roger Craig, forcing him to drop six passes; between us, we dropped ten passes during the game. The end result was that the Giants were the first team to prevent us from scoring a touchdown since the Chicago Bears did it in 1983. The Giants also did the impossible: They took our nose tackle Mike Carter out of the game. Joe Morris ran for 141 yards on twenty-eight carries. Phil Simms also had a good game, throwing thirty-one times for 181 yards. Despite the pain, I threw the ball forty-seven times, completing twenty-six passes for 296 yards.

The Giants believed we were looking past them to another matchup with Chicago, but that wasn't true. The 49ers' strategy has always been to take one game at a time. Bill knows that if we don't concentrate on the game at hand we won't go anywhere. We tried to handle the Giants even though we were hurting. The Giants were psyched. They put together a 34-yard drive in seven plays, ending in an Eric Schubert 47-yard field goal. In the second quarter Phil Simms took the Giants on a 38-yard drive in four plays. I set up their next score when Terry Kinnard intercepted a tipped pass and returned it to our 10-yard line. Phil wasted no time hitting Mark Bavaro—a Notre Dame alumnus—with a 15-yard touchdown pass, making the score 10–0.

We came right back, moving 85 yards in sixteen plays. The key plays on the drive were a 14-yard pass to Dwight and a 14-yard roughness penalty on Leonard Marshall. Moe kicked a 21-yard field goal, making the score 10–3 at the half.

I really took a beating in the first half. The Giants went right after my ribs. They delivered some late hits on me, including helping me up after a sack by trying to rip my arm out of my socket. The Giants also took aim at Roger's sore knee. The hits affected his concentration. Roger normally would have caught my swing passes. I guess he was shocked that he had dropped that many. Catfish finally pulled himself out of the game in the second half.

In the third quarter, the Giants put the game away, going 77 yards on eight plays. Phil hit Don Hasselbeck with a 3-yard pass, making the score 17–3. Our locker room looked like a M.A.S.H. unit following the game. I resembled a mummy, wrapped in a number of ace bandages with ice underneath. Roger's knees were iced down and covered with multiple bandages. The scene was typical of our entire season. We weren't able to keep people healthy, and if a team falls apart physically, the flow is interrupted. We had so many people missing during the season we couldn't put together a cohesive unit all year.

The Giants blew us out and believed they could beat the Bears. But that was not to be. I knew it was Chicago's year and they beat the Giants 21–0. I went to the Super Bowl to be honored before the game with the rest of the Super Bowl's Most Valuable Players. I had mixed emotions about going to New

Orleans for the game. It felt strange being there and not play-ing, but at the same time I was thrilled to be standing side by side with my idols Joe Namath and Len Dawson.

So it was a strange year for the 49ers. I hope we won't have to go through another season like that again. Believe me, it hurt.

Epilogue

The heat in Rocklin is about the only thing that never changes for a member of the San Francisco 49ers. When training camp rolls around there are going to be new faces and the same old routine. This year, a few things have changed. Freddie Solomon and Matt Cavanaugh, who was traded to Philadelphia, are gone, and things are not the same without them. Paul Hackett has moved on to coach with the Dallas Cowboys, and I'll miss him too.

The off-season has been a time to relax and reflect. Jen, Alexandra, and I went to Hawaii and Indonesia. The trips were interesting and helped me to get away from football, taking my mind off the game. Sitting here in the pool, I find myself reflecting again. Remember when I told you how I looked at my career in stages? I worked my way up to becoming a starter in high school and was knocked back down to the bottom in college. Well, I thought that process was all over when I became the 49ers' starting quarterback, but I was wrong. Now I know I will have to start all over again when I leave football and enter the real world. It's funny, I've spent a lot of time thinking about life after football; maybe it's because I turned thirty in June.

Don't get the idea I'm on the verge of retiring. I still have a long way to go, and I feel very good both mentally and physically.

Mom and Dad moved out here last spring, and it's great having the whole family together again. Watching the Pumpkin grow is fantastic and having Jen to share all this is such a tremendous feeling I really can't express it. All I can say is that I love her and she's changed my life. I'm settled, I feel relaxed both on and off the field. I'm a lucky man.

Not only lucky to have a wonderful family but lucky and grateful for having you, the fans. Yes, I know you don't hesitate to boo me, but that's your prerogative. Deep down inside I feel I've established a tremendous two-way relationship with the people of San Francisco and football fans across the country. Every one of you is special to me. I'm a performer and you have given me a lot of happiness and strength, feelings I'll always remember.

I'm grateful that you made the time and had the interest to listen to me. Now, if you'll excuse me, I'll just lie back in the pool and start thinking football. Who knows, maybe 1986 will be the 49ers' year. Take it easy.

—JOE MONTANA
Rocklin, California,
August 1986